## Zouti
## pou Gid

# Mentor
# Tools

## Herramientas
## de Mentor

## Equipping Global & Local
## Business Mentors

### Evan Keller

*Creating Jobs*.**org**
Business for Global Good

Creating Jobs Inc
DeLand, Florida

Mentor Tools: Equipping Global & Local Business Mentors

Published by:

Creating Jobs Inc

136 S. Sheridan Ave.

DeLand FL 32720

World Wide Web: www.creatingjobs.org

E-mail: info@creatingjobs.org

ISBN-10: 0-9967216-6-5

ISBN-13: 978-0-9967216-6-0

Printed in the United States of America

*As our trio moves on, I'm compelled to acknowledge the priceless teamwork of Chris Lumia and Kirk Harris. It's been a joyful five years as we've led this organization together. Your leadership on the board has enabled me to develop these tools in the field. Thank you Kirk for your careful guidance, and your love for people that flows from Our Father's love. Thank you Chris for your incisive wisdom, and your tireless work on unseen details which has enabled more visible works such as this. I'm forever grateful for how you two have indelibly shaped the soul of Creating Jobs Inc.*

# Table of Contents

## Part Three: LOCAL MENTORS | MENTORES LOCALES | GID LOKAL

## Part Four: INTERNATIONAL LEAD MENTORS | MENTORES PLOMO INTERNACIONALES | GID PRENSIPAL ENTÈNASYONAL

## Part Five: TRIP LOGISTICS | LOGÍSTICA VIAJE | PLANIFIKASYON POU VWAYAJ

## Part Six: BUSINESS AS MISSION | NEGOCIOS COMO MISIÓN | BIZNIS TANKOU MISYON

# Part One:

TRAINING

FORMACIÓN

FÒMASYON

# GrowBook Training Uses

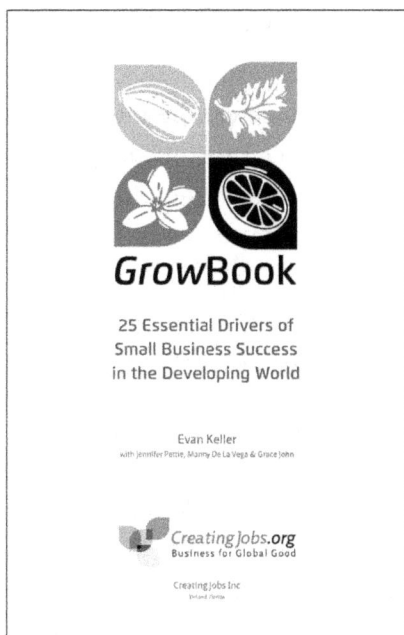

GrowBook

25 Essential Drivers of
Small Business Success
in the Developing World

Evan Keller
with Jennifer Pettie, Manny De La Vega & Grace John

CreatingJobs.org
Business for Global Good

Creating Jobs Inc

*Grow*Book is business training that has been honed in developing-world contexts, sharing a proven approach to growing successful small businesses.

## LEVEL TWO BUSINESS TRAINING:

GrowBook is designed for use by development organizations in their training of developing-world entrepreneurs. It is a level two course meant to compliment various introductory business curricula. GrowBook's 25 chapters easily adapt to training courses of various lengths. Of course, training is most effective when integrated with mentoring that presses application into individual businesses. Each chapter is organized into sections on What, Why, How, and Now

What. It's easy to follow, conducive for discussion, and practical to apply.

## TRAINING CONTEXTS:

GrowBook is designed to be taught as a single chapter per session course. This 25-session course can be taught once a month, once a week, or be compressed into a shorter timeframe as needed. Because the material is dense and action-oriented, it is best to allow time in between sessions to apply what is being learned.

## USE OF GROWBOOK ACTION PLAN:

We suggest that you have each participant use the Action Plan as a tool throughout the course. (The Action Plan is printed in GrowBook as well as in this book.) Use it as a pre-course self-assessment in which participants rate how mature their business is in each of the 25 session topics. During the course, they should use the Action Plan to record goals to pursue for each session. At the end of the course, participants should use the Action Plan to assess the progress they made during the course, and prioritize how they'll continue applying the course to their business.

## INTEGRATION WITH CAPITAL:

Microfinance institutions can use GrowBook to provide more training in their ongoing relationships with larger clients. Adding more intellectual capital will help clients get more mileage out of the financial capital they're receiving, become better clients, and grow stronger businesses which create more jobs and better serve their communities.

## MULTIPLE LANGUAGE EDITIONS:

Inexpensive ($12) paperbacks are available on Amazon.com in English, Spanish, and Haitian Creole. Upcoming editions include French and Mandarin, and we're open to exploring others with you. We'd like to make it as widely available as possible, so please let us know if you have a sizable interested population. If you can fund all or part of a translation, we can get it into your language of choice more quickly. To maximize impact for the glory of God, Creating Jobs Inc does not charge licensing fees for its use.

Inquire about using GrowBook in your context at: info@ creatingjobs.org

# Usos del GrowBook
# en Formación

Traducido por Cross Lingo

*Grow*Book es entrenamiento para negocios que ha sido perfeccionado en Latinoamérica, compartiendo un acercamiento acertado para el crecimiento de empresas pequeñas y medianas exitosas.

## CONSEJO PRÁCTICO PARA EL
## CRECIMIENTO DE NEGOCIOS:

Individualmente, los emprendedores pueden utilizar la sabiduría de GrowBook para construir un negocio más maduro. Es una guía para transformar un inicio con efectivo limitado y dependiente de su dueño, en una compañía exitosa con equipos de trabajo fuertes, utilidades crecientes y clientes devotos. Cada capítulo está organizado en secciones de referencia rápida sobre el Qué, Por Qué, Cómo y Ahora Qué. Es fácil de leer y puede ser aplicado en la práctica. Cubre todos los aspectos para el crecimiento de un negocio, ofreciendo pasos claros a tomar y casos de estudio de la vida real para ilustrarlos.

## CONTEXTOS DE ENTRENAMIENTO:

GrowBook está diseñado para ser enseñado como un curso de un capítulo a la vez. Este curso de 25 sesiones puede ser impartido una vez al mes, una vez a la semana o puede ser comprimido en espacios menores de tiempo según sea necesario. En vista que el material es denso y orientado a la acción, es mejor dejar tiempo entre sesiones para aplicar lo que está siendo aprendido.

## USO DEL PLAN DE ACCIÓN
## DEL GROWBOOK:

Sugerimos que haga que cada participante utilice el Plan de Acción como una herramienta a lo largo del curso. (El Plan de Acción está impreso en el GrowBook así como en este libro.) Utilícelo como una auto-evaluación previa al curso en la cual los participantes califican qué tan maduro es su negocio en cada uno de los temas de las 25 sesiones. Durante el curso, los participantes deberán utilizar el Plan de Acción para evaluar su progreso y priorizar cómo continuarán aplicando el curso en su negocio.

## ENTRENAMIENTO DE NEGOCIO NIVEL DOS:

Aparte del uso individual, GrowBook está diseñado como un currículo de entrenamiento para negocios. Es un curso nivel dos destinado a complementar varios curriculos introductorios de negocios. Los 25 capítulos de GrowBook se adaptan fácilmente a cursos de entrenamiento de distintas duraciones y son propicios para discusiones de grupo. Por supuesto, el entrenamiento es más efectivo cuando se integra con la mentoría que lleva a la aplicación individual en los negocios. No hay tarifa de licencia para su uso.

## INTEGRACIÓN CON MICROFINANZAS:

Las instituciones microfinancieras pueden utilizar GrowBook para proveer más entrenamiento en sus relaciones continuas con sus clientes más grandes. Añadir mayor capital intelectual ayudará a los clientes a obtener un mejor rendimiento del capital financiero que están recibiendo, a convertirse en mejores clientes y a crear más trabajos.

Consulte sobre el uso de GrowBook en su organización a: info@ creatingjobs.org

# Kouman yo sèvi ak GrowBook nan kou fòmasyon biznis.

Tradui pa Colibri Translation Services

GrowBook se yon fòmasyon biznis ki te pèfeksyone an Ayiti, ki pataje yon metodoloji epwouve pou devlope ti biznis ak biznis tay mwayen ki reyisi.

## KONSEY PRATIK POU DEVLOPE BIZNIS:

Antreprenè endividyèl kapab sèvi ak sajès ki genyen nan GrowBook pou devlope biznis ki pi mi. Liv sa a se yon gid pou transfòme yon jèn antrepriz ki pa gen anpil lajan e ki depann konplètman de pwopriyetè li a yon konpayi wobis ki gen yon ekip fò, pwofi kap grandi, ak kliyan ki fidèl. Chak chapit òganize an seksyon pou konsiltasyon rapid ki entitile Kisa, Poukisa, Kòman, ak E Kounyè a? Liv sa a fasil ni pou konprann ni pou mete an pratik. Li kouvri tout aspè devlope yon biznis, epi li bay etap pou pran ki klè ak etid de ka ki reyèl pou ilistre etap yo.

## KONTEKS FOMASYON:

Si nou pral ansenye GrowBook nan yon kou, chak sesyon kou a ta dwe kouvri yon sèl chapit. Ou kapab ansenye kou 25-sesyon sa a yon fwa chak mwa, yon fwa chak semèn, oubyen w kapab menm ansenye l nan yon peryòd tan ki pi kout selon le bezwen. Puiske chak chapit gen anpil enfòmasyon e anpil materyo etidyan an bezwen mete an pratik, li ta pi bon si w pèmèt etidyan yo ase tan ant sesyon yo pou yo mete sa y'ap aprann an pratik.

## KOMAN POU SEVI AK PLAN DAKSYON GROWBOOK LA:

Nou ta sijere w ankouraje chak moun ki patisipe pou li sèvi ak Plan Daksyon an pandan tout kou a. (Ou kapab jwenn Plan Daksyon an nan GrowBook e li nan liv sa tou.) Fè chak etidyan sèvi ak li anvan kou a konmanse pou li kapab evalye tèt li ak matirite biznis li a genyen nan chak nan 25 domèn yo ki pral kouvri pandan sesyon yo. Pandan kou a, se pou moun kap patisipe yo sèvi ak Plan Daksyon an pou ekri objektif yo ke yo ta renmen pousib apre chak sesyon. Nan fen kou a, se pou yo sèvi ak Plan Daksyon an pou evalye pwogrè yo te fè pandan kou a, e pou deside kisa yo bezwen mete an pratik an premye nan biznis yo.

## YON FOMASYON BIZNIS DEZYEM NIVO:

Nou pa te sèlman kreye GrowBook pou izaj endividyèl, men pou sèvi tou tankou tout yon pwogram ansèyman pou fòme moun nan biznis. Se yon kou dezyèm nivo li ye ki fèt pou konplimante lòt pwogram fòmasyon de baz. Venn senk (25) chapit GrowBook yo kapab adapte fasilman a kou pou fòmasyon nenpòt longè, e fòma konsiltasyon rapid la pwopis pou moun kap fè diskisyon nan gwoup. Fòmasyon sa a ap pi efikas si li jimle ak yon gid pèsonèl kap pouse moun mete sa yap aprann an pratik nan biznis pa yo. Pa gen okenn frè lisans ki bezwen peye pou sèvi ak liv sa a.

## ENTEGRASYON AK MIKWO-FINANSMAN:

Enstitisyon mikwo-finansman kapab sèvi ak GrowBook pou ofri plis fòmasyon antan yap devlope relasyon ak pi gwo kliyan yo. Kliyan kap ajoute plis kapital enteleksyèl ap pi efikas nan fason yo sèvi ak kapital finansye yap resevwa a, e ya tounen pi bon kliyan kap devlope biznis ki pi djanm, kap kreye plis anplwa, e kap sèvi komin yo pi byen.

Ou kapab mande ransèyman sou ki jan pouw sèvi ak GrowBook nan òganizasyon paw la nan: info@creatingjobs.org

# Guidelines for Curriculum Development

1.  Craft seminar topics in conjunction with recipients and in-country partner organizations, with the aim of catalyzing revenue growth, job creation, leadership development, and community renewal.

2.  Allow your work to be influenced by Creating Jobs Inc's vision, mission, and values.

3.  As you decide how much to present, allow for time to translate.

4.  Make careful efforts to "translate" your insights into the cultural context of the recipients.

5.  Bear in mind that we want to catalyze growth both in entrepreneurs and in their enterprises. Thus, we don't merely want to give directive instructions for them to implement; we'd rather invest in their minds so they make better decisions as leaders. For this reason, it is paramount to make them think, and help them to discover the "why" behind our recommendations. A great tool in spurring further reflection is to leave behind questions they can use to analyze their businesses according to the principles you've just taught.

6.  Without "dumbing down" your concepts, simplify your wording – especially idioms and technical terms – into phrases that are sure to translate well and be understood at the recipients' educational level. Give your translator advanced notice of any terms that may be difficult to translate. Give white board points to your translator in advance so he/she can do the written translation before the seminar.

7.  Prepare thoroughly, drawing on industry best practices,

relevant business literature, subject matter experts you have access to, and integrating these with your own knowledge and experience. Reduce your message down to a single idea and flesh it out with a handful of principles. Writing a purpose statement for your seminar is a great way to bring focus to your research. You may or may not state that purpose, but it should guide what is shared and how it's shared. This will help ensure that your seminar has a transformative result that really makes a difference in their thoughts and actions.

8.  Illustrate your principles with real-life examples from both your own business experience and from the successes you see in specific recipient businesses. This builds trust with your audience, connects with them, shows that you're paying attention to their work, honors their progress, helps them learn from each other, and helps them understand your principles from within their own world.

9.  Another surefire way to build trust and communicate effectively is to share your own mistakes related to your topic. Teaching by negative example is a memorable teaching method. It also can reinforce the entrepreneurial importance of risk-taking and greatness of failure as a teacher. It helps to frame you as a fallible human they can relate to.

10. With groups of 50 or less, it is important to engage them in discussion. A discussion question to draw out their insight on your topic roughly once every 15 minutes will help them stay engaged. With larger groups with which interaction doesn't seem appropriate, provide written discussion questions and time after your presentation for them to address them in pairs or table groups.

11. Leave your audience with handouts in their own language for their ongoing use. The potential for impact is greater than you may realize as your handout may be the ONLY resource on that topic that your audience will EVER read. Your audience

likely has limited access to quality business management materials, something we take for granted with the plethora of websites, magazines and books at our fingertips and within our budgets.

12. If possible, integrate your seminar training with your mentoring sessions so that they are mutually reinforcing. One way to do this is to go over the seminar handout and help them see how they could actually use it to apply the seminar principles to their business practices. In oral cultures or among those of limited education in any culture, using ideas on paper to make changes to behavior in real life is a foreign concept that requires ongoing reinforcement.

13. Follow well-known principles of effective communication, such as <u>Made to Stick</u>'s advice (by Chip & Dan Heath) that presentations should be: simple, unexpected, concrete, credible, emotional, and story-based. Being concrete is especially important in oral cultures where the audience may not be accustomed to sustained abstract thinking. Recipients have referenced diagrams as especially memorable.

14. Make your advice practical and easy to act upon. Be sure to give suggestions for application rather than making your content only cerebral. "When engaging in discussion or in a practical exercise, allow them to implement the concept learned to their specific business <u>right away</u>. The faster they can get "hands-on" the work, the more probability they will actually implement the new knowledge learned." – Debora Velis of Partners Worldwide in Honduras.

15. For most of our seminar topics, there are biblical principles that underpin the recommendations we make. Make the biblical directives or examples explicit and central in your presentation. Christian audiences will find it motivating, and Scripture is transformative for all types of audiences. Since our aim is not mere transfer of information, but actual transformation

of lives and communities, we'd be greatly amiss to omit the world's most powerful source of transformation. Our words of encouragement, the success stories we share, our positivity and friendliness can also powerfully inspire entrepreneurs to overcome adversity in growing their businesses.

# Presentation Tips

1. Stand as close as possible to your audience to communicate your eagerness to engage with them. Use body language, gestures and a friendly tone of voice to partially break the language barrier.

2. As you speak, look them in the eyes rather than looking at your translator.

3. Start your presentation with a sentence or two in their own language. Invest some time in deciding what to say and in memorizing it. This will make a far greater impact than you'd expect.

4. Thank your translator at beginning and end of your presentation.

5. Acknowledge hosts and other VIPs; these courtesies may be more important in this culture than in your own.

6. If there are direct quotations you'd like read, you can forego reading them in English to save time. Of course, give your translator the quotation ahead of time. Other tips for working effectively with an interpreter are found at: http://www.kwintessential.co.uk/translation/articles/interpreter.html

7. Express your confidence in them and your admiration of their courage in the face of adversity. Affirm their receptivity to mentoring and training.

# Part Two:

---

MENTORING

MENTORÍAS

SÈVI TANKOU GID

# GrowBook Mentoring Uses

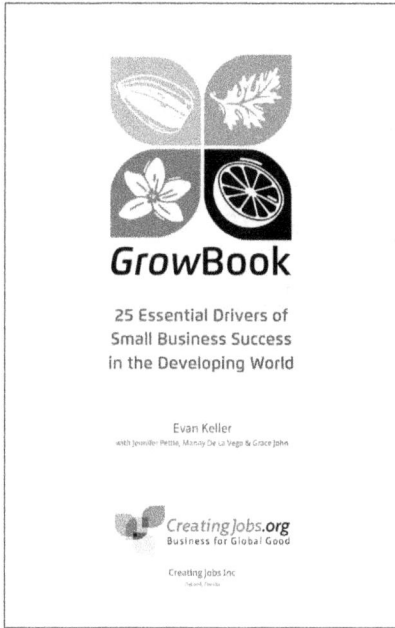

GrowBook is a 25-chapter book on how to grow a healthy business. Creating Jobs Inc wrote it for developing-world businesses and offers it in multiple languages on Amazon.com for only $12.

The best possible use for GrowBook is to have mentor-mentee pairs read a chapter per month, then discuss it together. They should come prepared to their meeting, ready to discuss challenges and opportunities to applying that chapter to the mentee's business. They should write goals during that meeting for how the mentee will apply the chapter in the coming month, discussing the results at their meeting the following month.

For mentor-mentee pairs that meet quarterly, entire "parts" of GrowBook should be read before the meeting and discussed together. GrowBook's 25 chapters are divided into these seven parts: Leadership, Market Position, Production, Sales & Service, Employees, Finance, and Giving Back. Applying a greater volume of content will be difficult, so mentors will need to help mentee's prioritize their goals. Another approach for quarterly meetings would be to discuss the single chapter which is most relevant to the entrepreneur's current challenges and opportunities.

Mentors should help mentors use the GrowBook Action Plan throughout the mentoring process to maximize positive results. It should be used as a self-assessment before reading GrowBook together, then again after all chapters have been discussed. It should be used throughout the process to set goals for each chapter and prioritize their pursuit.

# Usos del GrowBook en Mentorías

Traducido por Cross Lingo

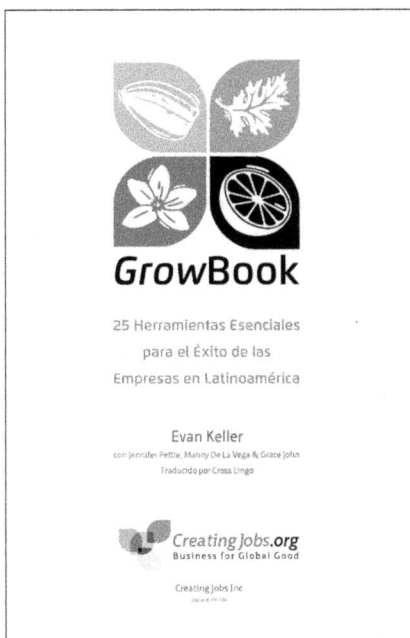

GrowBook

25 Herramientas Esenciales
para el Éxito de las
Empresas en Latinoamérica

Evan Keller
con Jennifer Pettie, Manny De La Vega & Grace John
Traducido por Cross Lingo

Creating Jobs.org
Business for Global Good

Creating Jobs Inc

GrowBook es un libro de 25 capítulos sobre cómo hacer crecer un negocio saludable. Creating Jobs Inc lo escribió para los negocios de los países en desarrollo y lo ofrece en múltiples idiomas en Amazon. com por tan solo $12.

Posiblemente, el mejor uso del GrowBook es hacer que las parejas mentor-aprendiz lean un capítulo al mes, y luego lo discutan juntos. Ambos deberían venir a su reunión preparados, listos para discutir los retos y oportunidades para aplicar ese capítulo en el negocio del aprendiz. Deberían escribir metas durante esa reunión sobre cómo el aprendiz aplicará el capítulo durante el siguiente mes, discutiendo así los resultados en su reunión del próximo mes.

Para las parejas mentor-aprendiz que se reúnen trimestralmente, "partes" enteras del GrowBook deberían ser leídas antes de la reunión y discutidas en conjunto. Los 25 capítulos del GrowBook están divididos en siete partes: Liderazgo, Posición de Mercado, Producción, Ventas & Servicio, Empleados, Finanzas y Dar. Aplicar un volumen más grande de contenido será difícil, así que los mentores necesitarán ayudar al aprendiz a priorizar sus metas. Otro enfoque para las reuniones trimestrales podría ser discutir el capítulo más relevante de acuerdo a los retos y oportunidades actuales del emprendedor.

Los mentores deben ayudarle a los aprendices a utilizar el Plan de Acción del GrowBook durante el proceso de mentoría para maximizar los resultados positivos. Debe ser utilizado como una auto-evaluación antes de leer juntos el GrowBook, luego otra vez después de haber discutido todos los capítulos. Debe ser utilizado a lo largo del proceso para definir metas para cada capítulo y priorizar su enfoque.

# Fason w Kapab Itilize GrowBook pou Sèvi Tankou yon Gid nan Biznis

Tradui pa Colibri Translation Services

GrowBook se yon liv ki gen 25 chapit ki pale de ki jan pou devlope yon biznis kap reyisi. Creating Jobs Inc te ekri liv sa pou biznis ki nan monn sou-devlope a e li vann li nan plizyè lang diferan sou Amazon.com pou $12 ameriken sèlman.

Pi bon fason pou itilize GrowBook se pou yon gid ak disip li nan biznis ta li yon chapit chak mwa e pale sou chapit la ansanm. Se pou yo vini nan reyinyon an tou prepare, prèt pou yo diskite tout defi ak opòtinite ki genyen pou mete chapit la an pratik nan biznis disip la. Yo ta dwe ekri plizyè objektif pandan y'ap reyini pou ki jan disip la va mete chapit la an pratik pandan mwa kap vini an, e yo kapab pale sou rezilta yo pandan pwochèn reyinyon yo apre yon lòt mwa.

Si yon gid ak disip li apral reyini chak trimès, se pou yo li tout yon pati nan liv GrowBook la anvan yo reyini pou yo kapab diskite li ansanm. GrowBook gen 25 chapit ki divize an sèt pati: Direksyon, Pozisyon sou Mache a, Pwodiksyon, Lavant ak Sèvis Kliyantèl, Anplwaye, Finans, ak Bay an Retou. Puiske lapral difisil pou mete plis materyo nan liv la an pratik a la fwa, gid la va bezwen ede disip li deside kilès nan objektif li yo ki pi enpòtan. Yon lòt apwòch yo kapab pran si yap reyini chak trimès se pou diskite sèlman chapit la ki pale plis sou defi ak opòtinite ki kanpe devan an antreprenè nan moman sa a.

Gid ta dwe ede disip sèvi ak Plan Daksyon GrowBook lan pandan tout pwosesis fòmasyon an pou yo reyalize pi bon rezilta. Se pou yo sèvi ak plan sa a tankou yon evalyasyon pou tèt yo dabò anvan yo li liv la ansanm, e se pou yo fè evalyasyon tèt yo ankò apre yo fin pale sou tout chapit yo. Se pou yo sèvi ak plan sa a pandan tout pwosesis fòmasyon an pou fikse objektif pou chak chapit e pou deside ki objektif ki pi enpòtan pou yo pousib.

# GrowBook
## Action Plan
by Evan Keller, November 2015

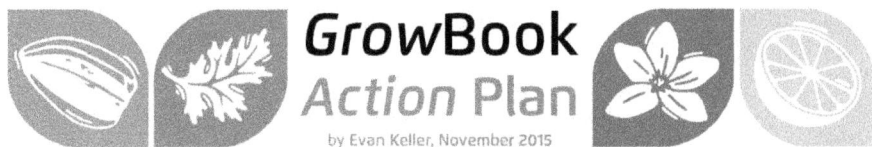

## How to use this tool:

**ASK** good questions, using the "Key" questions below and the "Assessment" and "Application" questions in each chapter of *Grow*Book.

**ASSESS** your growth toward each chapter's achievement, writing one of the following numbers in each box below: 5=Adult, 4=Young Adult, 3=Teen, 2=Child, 1=Infant. Add your scores and divide by 25 for your average maturity: $\Box \div 25 = \Box$. Note your strengths and weaknesses.

**PRIORITIZE** by identifying the top aspects of your business you need to work on over the next 12 months. Circle the chapters you want to focus on and update your priorities each quarter.

**PLAN** by writing goals for each priority.

**ACT** on your priorities *every* week.

## Part One | Leadership

☐ **1. Lead Yourself**

Key Question: Are you intentionally investing in your personal relationships, growth, and health?

Goals:

☐ **2. Set the Course**

Key Question: Have you written your company vision, mission, and values? Do you ensure everything else aligns with them?

Goals:

☐ **3. Pursue Goals**

Key Question: Have you written goals for this year and do you faithfully pursue them?

Goals:

☐ **4. Develop Systems**

Key Question: Do you write, implement, and improve employee processes to increase efficiency in your operations and consistency to your customers?

Goals:

☐ **5. Innovate Constantly**

Key Question: Are you always finding ways to improve your business?

Goals:

☐ **6. Overcome Fatalism**

Key Question: Do you believe the truth that you are empowered to positively shape your future?

Goals:

# Part Two | Market Position

☐ **7. Craft Customer-Focused Branding**

Key Question: Have you developed a name, tagline, and logo that speaks to your customers' needs and reveals your unique solutions?

Goals:

☐ **8. Generate a Sufficient Flow of Customers**

Key Question: Do you have a strong lead generation system? If not, are you spending considerable time pursuing potential customers?

Goals:

# Part Three | Production

☐ **9. Create Unique Customer Solutions**

Key Question: Do you provide unique solutions that people want and fit with your company identity? Do you make prototypes of new products and test them with some of your customers?

Goals:

☐ **10. Produce Efficiently**

Key Question: Are you working to improve the efficiency of your production so that you can please customers better and faster?

Goals:

# Part Four | Sales & Service

☐ **11. Close Sufficient High-Margin Sales**

Key Question: Do you build trusting relationships with your potential customers, communicating the value you offer and standing firm on your prices?

Goals:

☐ **12. Multiply Happy Customers**

Key Question: Do you consistently exceed your customers' expectations and go beyond what is required to fix your customer mistakes?

Goals:

# Part Five | Employees

☐ **13. Develop Sales, Production & Office Leaders**

Key Question: Have you been able to let go of these areas of responsibility and empower others to excel in them?

Goals:

☐ **14. Engage Employees**

Key Question: Have you built a positive company culture so that employees care about the company and their work?

Goals:

☐ **15. Build Teamwork**

Key Question: Are you developing team members and the team as a whole, helping them work together to achieve clear goals that align with your values?

Goals:

# Part Six | Finance

☐ **16. Achieve Positive Cash Flow**

Key Question: Are you practicing effective cash flow management, building systems to prevent future cash flow crises?

Goals:

☐ **17. Save Money Regularly**

Key Question: Are you regularly saving as much as you can in a separate account, patiently building financial strength?

Goals:

☐ **18. Control Spending Closely**

Key Question: Are you becoming more efficient by tracking your expenses and monitoring employee purchases?

Goals:

☐ **19. Negotiate Good Deals**

Key Question: Do you negotiate great deals by learning what is important to the other party, building trust, and seeking to achieve your top priorities while meeting some of theirs?

Goals:

☐ **20. Access Capital & Limit Debt**

Key Question: Are you gaining access to capital by being profitable, controlling debt, and providing documentation to lenders? Do you avoid unnecessary loans and pay down your loans as quickly as possible?

Goals:

☐ **21. Manage Major Risks**

Key Question: Have you identified and managed your major risks related to property, employees, and customers?

Goals:

☐ **22. Resist Corruption**

Key Question: Have you written policies and procedures so your employees know how to respond to unethical demands? Do you resist corruption even when it's costly?

Goals:

# Part Seven | Giving Back

☐ **23. Help Employees Grow**

Key Question: Are you intentionally helping employees grow their skills, maximize their strengths, and reach their aspirations?

Goals:

☐ **24. Mentor Other Entrepreneurs**

Key Question: Are you building trusting relationships with teachable entrepreneurs, offering thought-provoking questions, regular encouragement, and sound advice? Do you help them set and achieve goals for business growth and job creation?

Goals:

☐ **25. Serve with Time, Talent & Treasure**

Key Question: Are you leveraging your business and influence to serve your community? Do you use your profits and skills to make a difference in the world?

Goals:

# GrowBook
## Plan de Acción
por Evan Keller, traducido por Cross Lingo

## Cómo usar esta herramienta:

**EVALÚE** su crecimiento hacia alcanzar los logros en cada capítulo escribiendo uno de los siguientes números en las casillas correspondientes: 5=Adulto, 4=Adulto Joven, 3=Adolescente, 2=Niño, 1=Infante. Sume sus puntuaciones y divídalas por 25 para obtener su madurez promedio: □ ÷ 25 = □.

**REALICE** buenas peguntas, utilizando las preguntas "Claves" de abajo y las preguntas de "Evaluación" y "Aplicación" en cada capítulo de *Grow*Book. Esto revelará áreas de crecimiento.

**PRIORICE** los aspectos principales de su negocio en los cuales necesita trabajar en los siguientes 12 meses. Actualice sus prioridades cada trimestre.

**PLANIFIQUE** escribiendo metas para cada prioridad.

**ACCIONE** conforme a sus prioridades *cada* semana.

## Parte Uno | Liderazgo

□ **1. Auto-Lidérese**

Pregunta Clave: ¿Está invirtiendo intencionalmente en sus relaciones personales, en su salud y en su propio crecimiento?

Metas:

☐ **2. Establezca La Ruta**

Pregunta Clave: ¿Ha escrito la visión, misión y valores de su compañía? ¿Se asegura que todo lo demás esté alineado con ellas?

Metas:

☐ **3. Persiga Metas**

Pregunta Clave: ¿Ha escrito sus metas para este año y trabaja fielmente para alcanzarlas?

Metas:

☐ **4. Desarrolle Sistemas**

Pregunta Clave: ¿Usted escribe, implementa y mejora los procesos de los empleados para incrementar la eficiencia en sus operaciones y consistencia a sus clientes?

Metas:

☐ **5. Innove Constantemente**

Pregunta Clave: ¿Está siempre encontrando formas de mejorar su negocio?

Metas:

☐ **6. Supere el Fatalismo**

Pregunta Clave: ¿Usted cree la verdad de que usted está empoderado para moldear su futuro de forma positiva?

Metas:

# Parte Dos | Posición de Mercado

☐ **7. Mercadeo de marca Enfocado en el Cliente**

Pregunta Clave: ¿Ha desarrollado un nombre, eslogan y logo que le hable a las necesidades de sus clientes y revelen la solución única que usted ofrece?

Metas:

☐ **8. Genere Suficiente Flujo de Clientes**

Pregunta Clave: ¿Tiene un sistema fuerte de generación de oportunidades de venta? Si no lo tiene, ¿está invirtiendo una cantidad de tiempo considerable buscando clientes potenciales?

Metas:

# Parte Tres | Producción

☐ **9. Cree Soluciones Únicas para los Clientes**

Pregunta Clave ¿Provee usted soluciones únicas que las personas quieren y que encajan con la identidad de su compañía? ¿Hace prototipos de nuevos productos y los prueba con algunos de sus clientes?

Metas:

☐ **10. Produzca Eficientemente**

Pregunta Clave: ¿Está trabajando para mejorar la eficiencia de su producción de tal manera que usted pueda complacer mejor y de forma más rápida a sus clientes?

Metas:

# Parte Cuatro | Ventas & Servicio

☐ **11. Ventas con Margen lo Suficientemente Alto**

Pregunta Clave: ¿Construye relaciones de confianza con sus clientes potenciales, comunicándoles el valor de lo que usted ofrece y manteniendo firmemente sus precios?

Metas:

☐ **12. Multiplique los Clientes Felices**

Pregunta Clave: ¿Excede de manera consistente las expectativas de sus clientes y va más allá de lo requerido para enmendar errores con sus clientes?

Metas:

# Parte Cinco | Empleados

☐ **13. Desarrolle Líderes de Ventas, Producción & Oficina**

Pregunta Clave: ¿Ha podido delegar áreas de responsabilidad y ha empoderado a otros para que sobresalgan en las mismas?

Metas:

☐ **14. Involucre a los Empleados**

Pregunta Clave: ¿Ha construido una cultura empresarial positiva para que los empleados cuiden de la compañía y su trabajo?

Metas:

☐ **15. Construya Trabajo en Equipo**

Pregunta Clave: ¿Está desarrollando a los miembros del equipo y al equipo como tal, ayudándoles a trabajar en conjunto para lograr metas claras que estén alineadas con sus valores?

Metas:

# Parte Seis | Finanzas

☐ **16. Logre un Flujo de Efectivo Positivo**

Pregunta Clave: ¿Está practicando un manejo efectivo del flujo de caja, construyendo sistemas para prevenir crisis futuras de flujo de efectivo?

Metas:

☐ **17. Ahorre Dinero con Regularidad**

Pregunta Clave: ¿Está ahorrando tanto como pueda con regularidad y en una cuenta separada, pacientemente construyendo su fortaleza financiera?

Metas:

☐ **18. Controle los Gastos de Cerca**

Pregunta Clave: ¿Se está volviendo más eficiente, rastreando sus gastos y monitoreando las compras de sus empleados?

Metas:

☐ **19. Haga Buenas Negociaciones**

Pregunta Clave: ¿Realiza usted buenas negociaciones aprendiendo qué es importante para la otra parte, construyendo relaciones de confianza y buscando alcanzar sus metas principales mientras cumple con las de ellos?

Metas:

☐ **20. Acceso a Capital & Límite de Deuda**

Pregunta Clave: ¿Está ganando el acceso al capital para que su negocio sea rentable, poder controlar el endeudamiento y proveer documentación a los prestamistas? ¿Evita usted préstamos innecesarios y paga sus préstamos lo más rápido posible?

Metas:

☐ **21. Administre los Riesgos Principales**

Pregunta Clave: ¿Ha identificado y está administrando sus riesgos principales relacionados con su propiedad, empleados y clientes?

Metas:

☐ **22. Resista la Corrupción**

Pregunta Clave: ¿Ha escrito sus políticas y procedimientos para que sus empleados sepan cómo responder ante demandas no éticas? ¿Resiste la corrupción aún cuando pueda ser costoso?

Metas:

# Parte Siete | Dar

☐ **23. Ayude a los Empleados a Crecer**

Pregunta Clave: ¿Está intencionalmente ayudando a sus empleados a crecer en sus habilidades, maximizar sus fuerzas y alcanzar sus aspiraciones?

Metas:

☐ **24. Ofrezca Mentoría a Otros Emprendedores**

Pregunta Clave: ¿Está construyendo relaciones de confianza con emprendedores que sean enseñables, ofreciendo preguntas que estimulen el pensamiento, motivación constante y consejo sabio? ¿Les ayuda a definir y alcanzar sus metas para el crecimiento de su negocio y la creación de empleos?

Metas:

☐ **25. Sirva con Tiempo, Talento & Riquezas**

Pregunta Clave: ¿Está utilizando su negocio e influencia para servir a su comunidad? ¿Utiliza sus utilidades y habilidades para hacer la diferencia en el mundo?

Metas:

# GrowBook
## Plan Daksyon
pa Evan Keller, Novanm 2015

## Kòman pou sèvi ak zouti sa a:

**POZE** bòn kesyon. Sèvi ak kesyon « Kle » yo ki anba ak kesyon « Evalyasyon » e « Aplikasyon » nan chak chapit GrowBook.

**EVALYE** pwogrè w fè pou akonpli chak chapit. Ekri yonn nan chif suivan yo nan chak bwat anba: 5=Granmoun, 4=Jèn, 3=Adolesan, 2=Ti Moun, 1=Ti Bebe. Ajoute tout nòt ou yo e divize sòm nan pa 25 pou twouve matirite mwayèn ou: $\Box \div 25 = \Box$. Note fòs ak feblès ou yo.

**PRIYORIZE** aspè biznis ou a ou pi bezwen amelyore nan ane kap vini an. Ansèkle chapit yo ou ta renmen bay priyorite epi mete priyorite w yo a jou chak twa mwa.

**PLANIFYE** Ekri objektif pou chak dosye wap priyorize.

**AJI** sou priyorite w yo *chak* semèn.

## Premye Pati | Direksyon

☐ **1. Mennen Tèt Ou**

Kesyon Kle: Eske wap envesti entansyonèlman nan relasyon pèsonèl, devlopman ak sante w?

Objektif:

☐ **2. Trase Chimen An**

Kesyon Kle: Eske w deja ekri yon vizyon, misyon, ak valè pou konpayi w la? Eske wap asire ke tout lòt bagay nan konpayi w an akò ak dokiman sa yo?

Objektif:

☐ **3. Pousib Objektif**

Key Question: Eske w deja ekri objektif pou ane sa a e èske wap pousib yo fidèlman?

Objektif:

☐ **4. Devlope Sistèm**

Kesyon Kle: Eske w ekri, mete an pratik, e toujou chache amelyore pwosesis pou anplwaye w yo pou ogmante efikasite operasyon w lan e pou bay kliyan w yo menm eksperyans lan chak fwa?

Objektif:

☐ **5. Toujou ap Fè Bagay Tou Nèf**

Kesyon Kle: Eske wap toujou chache fason pou amelyore biznis ou?

Objektif:

☐ **6. Venk Lespri Fatalis La**

Kesyon Kle: Eske w kwè nan verite a — ke w gen puisans pou kreye yon lavni miyò?

Objektif:

## Dezyèm Pati | Pozisyon sou Mache a

☐ **7. Fasone yon Mak ki Fokalize sou Kliyan an**
Kesyon Kle: Eske w deja devlope yon non, slogan, e logo ki reponn a bezwen kliyan w yo e revele solisyon inik ou kapab bay yo?

Objektif:

☐ **8. Jwenn yon Bon Kantite Kliyan**
Kesyon Kle: Eske w gen yon bon sistèm pou kreye nouvo opòtinite? Sinon, èske wap pase anpil tan ap pousib kliyan potansyèl?

Objektif:

## Twazyèm Pati | Pwodiksyon

☐ **9. Kreye Solisyon pou Kliyan ki Inik**
Kesyon Kle: Eske w founi solisyon ki inik ke moun vle e ki an akò ak idantite konpayi w la? Eske w konn fè pwototip nouvo pwodui pou w kapab teste yo sou kèk nan kliyan w yo?

Objektif:

☐ **10. Pwodui ak Efikasite**
Kesyon Kle: Eske wap travay pou rann pwodiksyon w lan pi efikas pou w kapab fè kè kliyan w yo pi kontan pi vit?

Objektif:

# Katriyèm Pati | Lavant ak Sèvis Kliyantèl

☐ **11. Fè Ase Lavant Gwo Maj**

Kesyon Kle: Eske w devlope relasyon konfyans ak kliyan potansyèl ou yo? Eske w kominike yo valè ou kapab ofri yo, e èske w kanpe fèm sou pri w yo?

Objektif:

☐ **12. Bay Plis Kliyan Kè Kontan**

Kesyon Kle: Eske w toujou fè pi plis pase kliyan an tap tann? Si w lage kliyan an, èske w fè pi plis pase sak te nesesè pou ranje sa?

Objektif:

# Senkyèm Pati | Anplwaye

☐ **13. Devlope yon Ekip Lidè pou Lavant, Pwodiksyon ak Biwo**

Kesyon Kle: Eske w deja konmanse remèt domèn reskonsabilite sa yo nan men lòt moun? Eske w bay yo tout sa ki nesesè pou reyisi?

Objektif:

☐ **14. Angaje Pèsonèl La**

Kesyon Kle: Eske w kreye yon kilti pozitif nan konpayi w la pou rann anplwaye w yo sansib konpayi a ak travay yo a?

Objektif:

☐ **15. Travay an Ekip**

Kesyon Kle: Eske wap devlope ni manm ekip ou yo ni ekip ou a nan tout entegralite li? Eske wap ede yo travay ansanm pou acheve objektif ki klè e ki an akò ak valè w yo?

Objektif:

# Sizyèm Pati | Finans

☐ **16. Acheve yon Kach-Flo Pozitif**

Kesyon Kle: Eske wap jere kach-flo w la nan yon fason ki efikas? Eske w mete yon sistèm an plas pou prevni kriz nan kach-flo w la pi devan?

Objektif:

☐ **17. Toujou Sere Lajan**

Kesyon Kle: Eske w toujou sere tout lajan w kapab sere nan yon kont separe? Eske wap bati fòs finansyè w la ak pasyans?

Objektif:

☐ **18. Suiv Depans Ou Yo**

Kesyon Kle: Eske wap suiv depans ou yo ak acha anplwaye w yo ap fè pou w kapab pi efikas toujou?

Objektif:

☐ **19. Negosye Bon Zafè**

Kesyon Kle: Pou w kapab negosye bon zafè, èske w chache konnen sa ki pi enpòtan pou lòt pati a, bati konfyans ak li, e reyalize pi gran priyorite w yo anmenmtan ke w fè konpromi?

Objektif:

☐ **20. Jwenn Kapital e Limite Dèt**

Kesyon Kle: Eske wap jwenn aksè a kapital puiske w pwofitab, ou kontwole dèt ou, e ou founi tout dokiman pretè w yo bezwen? Eske w evite prete lajan lè sa pa nesesè e èske w repeye sa w prete a osi vit ke posib?

Objektif:

☐ **21. Jere Gwo Risk Yo**
Kesyon Kle: Eske w deja idantifye e jere pi gwo risk ou yo ki gen pou wè ak pwopriyete w, anplwaye w yo, ak kliyan w yo?

Objektif:

☐ **22. Reziste Koripsyon**
Kesyon Kle: Eske w genyen polis ak pwosedi ekri pou anplwaye w yo kapab konnen ki jan pou yo reponn a demann ki pa etik? Eske w reziste koripsyon menm si sa koute w chè?

Objektif:

## Setyèm Pati | Bay an Retou

☐ **23. Ede Anplwaye w Yo Grandi**
Kesyon Kle: Eske wap ede anplwaye w yo devlope konpetans yo, pèfeksyone fòs yo, e reyalize rèv yo?

Objektif:

☐ **24. Sèvi Tankou yon Gid pou Lòt Antreprenè**
Kesyon Kle: Eske wap devlope relasyon konfyans ak lòt antreprenè ki vle aprann nan men w? Eske w poze yo kesyon pou ensite yo reflechi, bay yo ankourajman, e ofri yo bon konsèy? Eske w ede yo fikse e reyalize objektif pou devlope biznis yo e kreye anplwa?

Objektif:

☐ **25. Sèvi Lòt Moun ak Tan, Talan e Trezò Ou**
Kesyon Kle: Eske w sèvi ak biznis e enfliyans ou pou sèvi kominote w la? Eske w itilize pwofi w ak konpetans ou yo pou rann monn sa miyò?

Objektif:

# Top 20 Best Practices of International Mentors

1. **Select Winners**: Work with the in-country partner organization to identify high capacity entrepreneurs. Accept them into the program only after visiting their businesses and interviewing them using questions from our <u>Screening Prospective Mentees</u> document.

2. **Explain the Program**: Share what you hope they'll gain from the program, seeing if they're willing to commit to the parameters and expectations outlined on our <u>Program Fact Sheet</u>. Provide translated versions of the fact sheet and our <u>Foundational Documents</u> (vision/mission) laminated inside a notebook you give them for their note-taking during mentoring sessions.

3. **Be a Friend**: Build strong personal connections with the entrepreneurs you serve, especially through asking about their families and spending informal time with them outside the mentoring sessions. Bonding with them through soccer games has been especially fun, eliciting friendly bantering and leveling the power equation with those of us who don't play much soccer. Joining their families at the beach, over lunch or in church has been great as well. During the mentoring sessions, share your own joys and struggles in family and business and offer to pray for them.

4. **Provide Continuity**: If you have a rotating team of mentors, always send someone who the entrepreneurs have met before to provide continuity in the relationship. I recommend a "lead mentor" who leads each mentor visit, bringing one or two (at the most) mentors with complementary skills and experience. Any more than three will make the cross-lingual conversation

too chaotic, over-crowd the entrepreneur's office, and require a second vehicle. Partners Worldwide has honed this model well over the years.

5.  **Use Their Language**: Learn and use basic phrases in their language. This builds on the personal connection, showing that you value their culture and have invested effort to show them you care. It also gives you an opportunity to directly learn from them. For Haiti, feel free to use our <u>Creole Phrase Guide</u>.

6.  **Relinquish Control**: Allow their felt needs to direct the conversation: "What would you like to discuss today?" Ask them early in each mentoring session what opportunities and challenges they're currently facing in their business.

7.  **Use *Grow*Book and its Action Plan**. Discuss one chapter of GrowBook per month with your mentees, helping them apply it to their businesses. Help mentees assess the maturity of their businesses using the GrowBook Action Plan. Help them choose a few areas to work on over the next three months and set related goals.

8.  **Establish Goals**: Agree on goals for the relationship, such as "grow companies, create jobs, and help communities thrive" (our mission).

9.  **Encourage Community Service**: Help them to leverage their businesses to serve their communities, in keeping with our vision of "business for global good". Encourage community investment that is both intrinsic (through their goods, services, jobs and re-circulated revenue) and instrumental (through their relationships, time, influence and profits). Start by asking "What community needs do you care about?"

10. **Develop Local Mentors**: Envision them to mentor other entrepreneurs during and after receiving mentorship,

suggesting our <u>Locals Mentoring Locals</u> as a simple guide. Locals investing in locals is an essential key to sustainability. As they become local mentors and their businesses become stronger, you could spend less time discussing their own businesses and more on coaching their coaching. Those who naturally share their business acumen with others should be encouraged to make their mentoring more intentional and systematic. We must *inspire* them to see the impact they could make, and *simplify* a process which seems mystifying to some. Those who think mentoring is too difficult and better left to Americans should be encouraged that it's simply passing on what they already know. They've already done the hard part – starting and growing a successful business. Mentoring simply leverages those hard-won lessons for further good. Use our <u>Local Mentor Program</u> as a guide to recruit, train and support local mentors.

11. **Build Capacity**: Focus on both developing capacity of the entrepreneurs as well as coaching towards business growth. We want to grow their ability to make good decisions on their own in the future while being wise in how they run their business today. Managing this tension is a delicate dance. We want to build businesses, but more importantly, build people.

12. **Write Mentee Recommendations**: Offer written, translated recommendations after each mentoring session, for their own growth as leaders as well as ideas to grow their businesses.

13. **Write Mentor Recommendations**: Write recommendations for yourselves as well, and be sure to follow up to provide the connections and resources you've promised. This shows that you don't forget about them when you're at home.

14. **Seek In-Country Follow Up**: Ask the in-country partner organization to visit each entrepreneur roughly halfway in between your quarterly Mentor Visits. Ask if they would deliver your written recommendations, contextualize them to

the local culture, and find out which of the recommendations the entrepreneurs want to create goals around. Our <u>Follow Up Form</u> could be used in these meetings and emailed to you afterwards along with a current profit and loss statement. Effective follow up can multiply our efforts, help us prepare better, and provide essential encouragement and accountability to the entrepreneurs. Reciprocate by being a good partner, fulfilling agreed upon partnership expectations.

15. **Train**: Provide a training seminar on each mentor visit on issues they're currently facing. Choose one of 25 chapters from GrowBook, which is written as a business training curriculum. It should only take a few minutes to adapt any chapter to your audience. This maximizes your impact and offers deeper and more thoughtful advice. When developing your own curriculum, check out our <u>Guidelines for Curriculum Development</u>.

16. **Encourage Mutual Support**: Encourage entrepreneurs to meet monthly to encourage and support each other. Doing business with each other and being intentional in their teamwork multiplies their ability to help their communities thrive. A simple format for such a meeting can center on a question like "How are you growing your business and making it a force for good?" Or it can focus on peer coaching in which an entrepreneur's current challenge is tackled together. This will do wonders in building a stronger sense of community and group identity.

17. **Transition Quickly**: Craft an exit strategy. As entrepreneurs approach the end of your program's term (2-3 years), you can build the expectation that they'll either graduate from the program or receive ongoing mentoring as they transition from mentee to mentor. Expect a 25% dropout rate as some won't be open to advice or see value in the program. The quicker you can identify these and provide a shame-free exit,

the sooner you can invest in others with higher capacity and motivation to create jobs. If they break appointments for their mentoring sessions with you, the arrangement can be allowed to naturally fade away. You can "graduate" others, saying that their business no longer needs quarterly input from you, but that you'd be glad to catch up with them over lunch on future visits. Ask your in-country partners for insight into the cross-cultural relational dynamic, and for advice on culturally-appropriate ways to wrap up the mentoring relationship.

18. **Be Positive**: Always find something in their work to compliment; your encouragement and affirmation can have a lasting impact.

19. **Capture Stories**: With permission, take short videos that give a quick overview of the entrepreneur's opportunities and challenges in business, highlighting how your coaching has made a difference. Take close up photos of entrepreneurs with their products and/or employees. Take time to succinctly write down the top stories.

20. **Recruit New Mentors**: Share stories and images from each trip with potential mentors back home. Keep in mind that it usually takes over a year to successfully recruit a new mentor, so keep many strong prospects in the pipeline and nurture them consistently. See our <u>Mentor Recruiting Steps</u>.

# Sample Mentoring Session

Exchange warm greetings in their own language.

Find a quiet place to sit, if possible.

Ask and share about families.

Ask and share about businesses.

Share any resources you've researched for them.

Ask "What would you like to discuss today?"

Analyze their latest financial reports together.

Record current job count.

Ask "How did you do towards accomplishing your goals for the last three months?" Look over their GrowBook Action Plan with them, helping them to identify areas in which they'd like to grow in the upcoming quarter, and setting specific goals in those areas. Write those goals on your copy of their Action Plan while they do the same on theirs. Suggest pertinent GrowBook chapters for them to read.

Offer your top three recommendations and ask them to write down their top three goals for the next three months.

Record them yourself and let them know that your in-country partners will follow up on their progress before your next visit. Let them know when you or other mentors will come again.

Discuss at least one aspect of local mentorship: its importance and their ability as a mentor, their progress towards becoming a local mentor, a simple process to begin, their growth as a mentor, or the challenges and opportunities of their mentees.

Discuss ways they can leverage their business to serve the community.

Invite them to any business training that is available.

End with affirmation for the positive things you're seeing and offer to pray for their business.

With permission, take a photo which captures a story (mentoring scene with eye contact between participants, new employee you interview, new product/packaging/sign/manager).

## Notes:

When not able to cover all of the above in two hours, discern what is important for this session. Be flexible and open to the conversation going in a direction you didn't foresee. Often a single topic will take center stage, which increases retention and impact - especially in an oral culture. Make sure the entrepreneur has space to discuss all they'd like to talk about, even if it upends this conversation guide!

If you have a co-mentor with you, ask him/her to watch the time and tell you 10 minutes before you need to leave so can cover essential items.

When appropriate, ask the entrepreneur if a manager or key employee should join part of conversation. In some cultures, entrepreneurs are very guarded when speaking about their business in front of their employees, so ask any financial or otherwise sensitive question when no employees are present.

Whenever possible, encourage connections between entrepreneurs (to do business together, meet regularly for mutual support, enjoy lunch or recreation together with you).

So that your next visit builds on this one, take good notes either using the Mentoring Guide or GrowBook Action Plan.
Refer to what you learned from the recent Follow-up Form (from local partner visit since your last visit).

Sometimes it's necessary to discuss the program - explaining it in the first two sessions (using Program Fact Sheet) then occasionally getting feedback on how it can be made more helpful for them.

Don't forget to listen! When entrepreneur and translator are going back and forth, it's easy to forge ahead with your next point and miss what's really going on.

# Ejemplo de Sesión de Mentoría

Traducido por Cross Lingo

Intercambien saludos cálidos en su propio idioma.

De ser posible, encuentre un lugar callado donde sentarse.

Pregunten y compartan acerca de las familias.

Pregunten y compartan acerca de los negocios.

Comparta cualquier recurso o información que usted haya investigado para ellos.

Pregunte "¿Qué le gustaría discutir el día de hoy?"

Analice junto al aprendiz sus últimos estados financieros.

Registre la cantidad actual de empleos.

Pregunte, "¿Cómo le fue alcanzando sus metas en los últimos tres meses?" Analice junto al aprendiz su Plan de Acción del GrowBook, ayudándole a identificar áreas en las que les gustaría crecer en el siguiente trimestre, y definir metas específicas en esas áreas. Escriba esas metas en su copia del Plan de Acción al mismo tiempo que él las escriben en su plan. Sugiera capítulos del Growbook que sean pertinentes para que lea.

Ofrézcale tres recomendaciones primordiales y pídales que escriban sus tres metas principales para los próximos tres meses.

Regístrelas usted mismo y hágales saber que sus socios en el país darán seguimiento en su progreso previo a su siguiente visita. Hágales saber cuándo volverá a venir usted u otros mentores.

Discuta al menos un aspecto sobre la mentoría local; su importancia y habilidad como un mentor, el progreso hacia convertirse en un mentor local, un proceso simple para comenzar, su crecimiento como mentor, o los retos y oportunidades de sus aprendices.

Discuta formas en las que él puede aprovechar su negocio para servir a la comunidad.

Invítelos a cualquier entrenamiento de negocio que esté disponible.

Finalice afirmándolos con las cosas positivas que usted está viendo y ofrézcales orar por su negocio.

Con su autorización, tome una foto que capture una historia (la sesión de mentoría con contacto visual entre los participantes, la entrevista a un nuevo empleado, nuevo producto/empaque/rótulo/ administrador).

## Notas:

Cuando no pueda abarcar todo lo anterior en dos horas, discierna qué es importante para esta sesión. Sea flexible y abierto a que la conversación tome una dirección que usted no haya previsto. A menudo un tema en particular tomará la atención principal, lo cual incrementa la retención e impacto - específicamente en una cultura oral. Asegúrese que el emprendedor tenga espacio para discutir todo lo que a él le gustaría hablar, incluso si difiere con esta guía conversacional.

Si usted tiene un co-mentor con usted, pídale a él/ella que preste atención al tiempo y le avise cuando resten 10 minutos antes de irse, así usted podrá asegurarse de cubrir los elementos esenciales.

Cuando sea apropiado, pregúntele al emprendedor si un administrador o empleado clave debería participar en la conversación. En algunas culturas, los emprendedores son muy reservados cuando hablan acerca de su negocio enfrente de sus empleados, así que realice cualquier pregunta financiera o sensitiva cuando no estén los empleados presentes.

Cuando sea posible, estimule las conexiones entre los emprendedores (para hacer negocio entre ellos, reunirse con regularidad para apoyo mutuo, almorzar o tener tiempo recreacional junto con usted).

Para lograr que la próxima visita sea una continuación de ésta, tome buenas notas ya sea utilizando la Guía para Mentor o el Plan de Acción del GrowBook.

Remítase a lo que usted aprendió del Formulario de Seguimiento (de la visita del socio local posterior a su última visita).

A veces es necesario discutir el programa - explicarlo en las primeras dos sesiones (utilizando la Hoja de Aspectos del Programa) y luego obtener ocasionalmente retroalimentación sobre cómo se puede mejorar para que sea de más ayuda para ellos.

¡No olvide escuchar! Cuando el emprendedor y el traductor están interactuando, es fácil que usted se mueva al siguiente punto y que ignore lo que realmente está sucediendo.

# Echantiyon yon Sesyon Fòmasyon Gid

Tradui pa Colibri Translation Services

Salye moun yo byen nan pwòp lang pa yo.

Chache yon kote trankil pou nou chita, si sa posib.

Poze keksyon e pataje sou fanmi nou yo.

Poze keksyon e pataje sou biznis nou yo.

Pataje nenpòt resous ou te chache pou yo.

Mande yo « Sou kisa w ta renmen pale jodi a?

Analize dènye rapò finansyè yo ansanm.

Ekri konbyen anplwaye yo genyen aktyèlman.

Mande yo « Ki pwogrè w te fè sou objektif ou yo pandan dènye twa mwa yo? » Revize Plan Daksyon GrowBook yo a ansanm ak yo, epi ede yo idantifye ki kote yo ta renmen grandi nan trimès kap vini an. Fikse objektif spesifik nan domèn sa yo. Ekri objektif sa yo sou kopi pa w de Plan Daksyon an e fè yo ekri menm bagay la sou kopi pa yo. Sijere yo kèk chapit pou yo li nan liv GrowBook ki ta pètinan a objektif sa yo.

Ofri twa pi gran rekòmandasyon w yo epi mande yo ekri twa pi gran objektif pa yo pou trimès kap vini an.
Anrejistre objektif yo nan kopi pa w e fè yo konprann ke patnè

lokal ou yo va fè suivi sou pwogrè yo anvan nou reyini ankò. Fè yo konnen ki lè yo va wè ou menm ou byen yon lòt gid ankò.

Pale sou o mwens yon aspè de sèvi tankou yon gid lokal: enpòtans relasyon gid la genyen, kapasite yo genyen kòm gid, e pwogrè yo fè nan sèvi tankou yon gid, yon pwosesis senp pou konmanse, ou defi ak opòtinite yo ki fè fas ak disip yo.

Pale de plizyè fason yo kapab itilize biznis yo pou sèvi kominote yo a.

Envite yo nan evènman pou fòmasyon biznis, si sa disponib.

Klotire ak yon afimasyon de tout bagay pozitif ke ou wè nan biznis yo e ofri pou w priye pou biznis yo.

Ak pèmisyon yo, fè yon foto ki rakonte yon istwa (pa egzanp, fè yon foto de yon gid ak yon disip kap gade yonn ak lòt nan je pandan yon reyinyon, oubyen yon nouvo anplwaye kap fè entèvyou, oubyen yon nouvo produi/anbalaj/ansèy/manedjè).

## Nòt:

Si nou pa kapab kouvri tout sa ki ekri anwo a nan dezèdtan, deside kisa ki pi enpòtan pou nou kouvri pandan sesyon sa a. Se pou w fleksib e se pou w dakò kite konvèsasyon an ale nan direksyon ou pat prevwa. Souvan se yon sèl dosye ki vin domine tout konvèsasyon an, men sa ka ogmante enpak konvèsasyon an genyen e li kapab ede lòt moun nan chonje pi byen kisa nou te di - sitou nan yon kilti oral. Asire w ke antreprenè a gen ase libète pou pale sou tout sa ki konsène li, menm si sa vle di konvèsasyon nou an pa koresponn ak gid konvèsasyon an ki ekri anwo!

Si w genyen yon lòt gid la ansanm avè w, mande li veye lè a e fè w konnen lè gen 10 minit ki rete anvan w bezwen ale. Konsa, n'ap ka kouvri tout sa nou bezwen kouvri.

Lè sa posib, mande antreprenè a si yon manedjè ou yon anplwaye kle ta dwe prezan pou konvèsasyon an. Nan kèk kilti, antreprenè pa renmen pale de zafè yo devan anplwaye yo, donk pa poze keksyon sou dosye finans ou sou lòt dosye konfidansyèl si gen anplwaye ki prezan.

Nenpòt lè sa posib, ankouraje antreprenè fè lyezon ant yo menm kote yap reyini regilyèman pou sipòte yonn ak lòt oubyen manje ou patisipe nan lòt amizman ni ant yo menm ni avèk ou menm.
Pou w kapab kontinye devlope nan pwochèn reyinyon nou an sa nou te konmanse devlope nan reyinyon sa a, pran bon nòt. Ou kapab itilize Gid pou Gid Biznis la oubyen Plan Daksyon GrowBook la pou ede w fè sa.

Fè referans a sa w te aprann de dènye Fòmilè de Suivi a (ki te distribye nan reyinyon patnè lokal yo depi dènye fwa w te la).

Pafwa li vin nesesè pou w esplike kisa Pwogram la ye - ou kapab esplike li nan premye de sesyon yo (ou kapab itilize Fèy Enfòmasyon Pwogram lan pou ede w fè sa) epi w kapab chache reyaksyon lòt moun nan sou ki jan pwosesis la kapab amelyore.

Pa bliye koute yo! Lè yon antreprenè ak yon entèprèt ap pale, li fasil pou w pouse pou pi devan ak pwochen pwen w vle fè a e pou w manke wè yon bagay ki vrèman enpòtan.

# Mentoring Report

| | |
|---|---|
| Mentoring Report For: | |
| Owner: | |
| Date: | |
| Author: | |
| Creating Jobs Inc Members who visited: | |
| Local Mentor Assigned to this Business: | |

**LONG TERM VISION:**



**STRATEGY:**



**FINANCIAL STATUS AND METRICS:**

| | |
|---|---|
| Jobs Created since last visist: | |
| Jobs Retained: | |
| Sales Increased or Decreased compaired to last period: | |

Additional Notes:

## AREAS OF FOCUS ON THEIR GROWBOOK ACTION PLAN:

## ACTIONS ITEMS FOR MENTEES (TO BE REVIEWED BY CREATING JOBS INC ON NEXT VISIT):

## ACTION ITEMS FOR MENTORS:

## QUESTIONS TO BE ASKED BY CREATING JOBS INC ON NEXT VISIT:

1.

## NEW FACTS GATHERED ON THIS VISIT:

## ACCUMULATED KNOWLEDGE:

# Follow Up Form

Entrepreneur's Name:

Business Name:

Author of Report:

Date of Report:

<u>Please deliver and explain the most recent translated business recommendations from Creating Jobs Inc.</u>

Recommendations that entrepreneur would like to commit to, with timeline to start/finish each one:

Progress entrepreneur has made on goals he/she has set on his GrowBook Action Plan:

New developments in the business since last Creating Jobs' Mentor Visit:

Issues entrepreneur would like to discuss with mentors:

How entrepreneur is working to grow his/her company, create jobs, and serve his/her community:

Please attach most recent profit & loss statement.

# Hoja de Seguimiento

Nombre del Empresario:

Nombre de la Empresa:

Autor del Reporte:

Fechas del Reporte:

<u>Por favor comparta y explica las recomendaciones traducidas mas recientes de Creating Jobs Inc.</u>

Recomendaciones a las que el emprendedor le gustaría comprometerse, con la fecha de inicio y fecha en que la terminara:

Empresario Progreso ha hecho en las metas que él / ella ha establecido en su GrowBook Plan de Acción:

Nuevos cambios en la empresa desde la última visita de Creating Jobs Inc.:

Asuntos que el empresario le gustaría discutir más a fondo con los mentores:

Como el emprendedor está trabajando para crecer su empresa, crear empleos y servir a su comunidad:

Adjuntar el más actual estado de resultados.

# Scriptures with Powerful Business Applications

Exodus 18:13-26

[13] The next day Moses took his seat to serve as judge for the people, and they stood around him from morning till evening. 14 When his father-in-law saw all that Moses was doing for the people, he said, "What is this you are doing for the people? Why do you alone sit as judge, while all these people stand around you from morning till evening?"

[15] Moses answered him, "Because the people come to me to seek God's will. [16] Whenever they have a dispute, it is brought to me, and I decide between the parties and inform them of God's decrees and instructions."

[17] Moses' father-in-law replied, "What you are doing is not good. [18] You and these people who come to you will only wear yourselves out. The work is too heavy for you; you cannot handle it alone. [19] Listen now to me and I will give you some advice, and may God be with you. You must be the people's representative before God and bring their disputes to him. [20] Teach them his decrees and instructions, and show them the way they are to live and how they are to behave. [21] But select capable men from all the people—men who fear God, trustworthy men who hate dishonest gain—and appoint them as officials over thousands, hundreds, fifties and tens. [22] Have them serve as judges for the people at all times, but have them bring every difficult case to you; the simple cases they can decide themselves. That will make your load lighter,

because they will share it with you. [23] If you do this and God so commands, you will be able to stand the strain, and all these people will go home satisfied."

[24] Moses listened to his father-in-law and did everything he said. [25] He chose capable men from all Israel and made them leaders of the people, officials over thousands, hundreds, fifties and tens. [26] They served as judges for the people at all times. The difficult cases they brought to Moses, but the simple ones they decided themselves.

Deuteronomy 8:18
'But remember the LORD your God, for it is he who gives you the ability to produce wealth.'

Here's what Bob Lupton says about this verse:
"Wealth creation is a gift of the Creator - a spiritual gift.
I have often heard sermons on the seductiveness of wealth, but I have yet to hear a sermon affirming the spiritual gift of wealth-creation.
And yet it is this very gift that enables our society to flourish.
And it is this gift that holds the key to the alleviation of poverty."

Nehemiah 6 –When Sanballat threatened Nehemiah's life to derail his rebuilding of Jerusalem's wall, he proclaimed emphatically: "I am doing a great work", "I cannot [be destracted]", I will not [hide to save my life]". Instead, he prayed: "But now, O God, strengthen my hands." When he completed the wall, Israel's enemies "recognized that this work had been accomplished with the help of our God." As we step out in faith to fulfill our Kingdom callings, God strengthens us and it is seen that God has been at work in our work for his glory.

Psalm 37:21

[21] The wicked borrow and do not repay,
but the righteous give generously;

Psalm 127:1-2
1 Unless the Lord builds the house,
the builders labor in vain.
Unless the Lord watches over the city,
the guards stand watch in vain.
2 In vain you rise early
and stay up late,
toiling for food to eat—
for he grants sleep to[a] those he loves.

Proverbs 11:10-11:
When the righteous prosper, the city rejoices; when
the wicked perish, there are shouts of joy. Through the
blessing of the upright a city is exalted, but by the mouth
of the wicked it is destroyed.

Proverbs 14:4, New American Standard Version
Where no oxen are, the manger is clean, But much revenue
comes by the strength of the ox.

Barnes Notes on the Bible: "Labor has its rough, unpleasant side,
yet it ends in profit. So also, the life of contemplation may seem
purer, "cleaner "than that of action. The outer business of the world
brings its cares and disturbances, but also "much increase." There
will be a sure reward of that activity in good works for him who
goes, as with "the strength of the ox," to the task to which God calls
him."

In other words, business brings both trouble and benefit.

Proverbs 14:23 New American Standard Version

In all labor there is profit, but mere talk leads only to poverty.

Proverbs 15:22
Plans fail for lack of counsel, but with many advisers they succeed.

Proverbs 18:9
One who is slack in his work is brother to one who destroys.

Proverbs 21:5, New International Version
The plans of the diligent lead to profit as surely as haste leads to poverty.

Proverbs 21:5, New Living Translation
Good planning and hard work lead to prosperity, but hasty shortcuts lead to poverty.

Proverbs 22:7, New International Version
The rich rule over the poor, and the borrower is slave to the lender.

Proverbs 24:5-6
5 A wise man has great power, and a man of knowledge increases strength; 6 for waging war you need guidance, and for victory many advisers.

Proverbs 24:16
"Though *a righteous man falls seven times*, he will get up."

Proverbs 24:19-20
19 Do not fret because of evildoers
or be envious of the wicked,
20 for the evildoer has no future hope,

and the lamp of the wicked will be snuffed out.

Another translation says "do not be overly upset with evildoers". Great word for business since it seems to draw so many who want to cheat us! Why should we give them so much power over us... their days are numbered and so is their evil. We pity not fear them.

Proverbs 27:23, New International Version
Be sure you know the condition of your flocks, give careful attention to your herds;

Proverbs 30:25
Ants are creatures of little strength, yet they store up their food in the summer;

Proverbs 31
[Look up entire chapter.]

Ecclesiastes 10:10, New American Standard Version
If the axe is dull and he does not sharpen its edge, then he must exert more strength. Wisdom has the advantage of giving success.

Ecclesiastes 11:4
He who observes the wind will not sow, and he who regards the clouds will not reap.

Jeremiah 15:21
I will deliver you out of the hand of the wicked, and redeem you from the grasp of the ruthless."

Jeremiah 22:13-16
13 "Woe to him who builds his palace by unrighteousness, his upper rooms by injustice,
making his own people work for nothing,

not paying them for their labor.
<sup>14</sup> He says, 'I will build myself a great palace
with spacious upper rooms.'
So he makes large windows in it,
panels it with cedar
and decorates it in red.

<sup>15</sup> "Does it make you a king
to have more and more cedar?
Did not your father have food and drink?
He did what was right and just,
so all went well with him.
<sup>16</sup> He defended the cause of the poor and needy,
and so all went well.
Is that not what it means to know me?"
declares the LORD.

Matthew 7:12
<sup>12</sup> So in everything, do to others what you would have them
do to you, for this sums up the Law and the Prophets.

Matthew 25:20-21, New Living Translation
<sup>20</sup> The servant to whom he had entrusted the five bags of
silver came forward with five more and said, 'Master, you
gave me five bags of silver to invest, and I have earned
five more.'

<sup>21</sup> "The master was full of praise. 'Well done, my good
and faithful servant. You have been faithful in handling
this small amount, so now I will give you many more
responsibilities. Let's celebrate together!'

2 Corinthians 9:6-11, New International Version
<sup>6</sup> Remember this: Whoever sows sparingly will also reap
sparingly, and whoever sows generously will also reap

generously. 7 Each of you should give what you have decided in your heart to give, not reluctantly or under compulsion, for God loves a cheerful giver. 8 And God is able to bless you abundantly, so that in all things at all times, having all that you need, you will abound in every good work. 9 As it is written:

"They have freely scattered their gifts to the poor; their righteousness endures forever." [a]

10 Now he who supplies seed to the sower and bread for food will also supply and increase your store of seed and will enlarge the harvest of your righteousness. 11 You will be enriched in every way so that you can be generous on every occasion, and through us your generosity will result in thanksgiving to God.

Ephesians 5:15-16
15 Be very careful, then, how you live—not as unwise but as wise, 16 making the most of every opportunity, because the days are evil.

Colossians 3:23
Whatever you do, work at it with all your heart, as working for the Lord, not for human masters,

2 Thessalonians 1:11, New Living Translation
So we keep on praying for you, asking our God to enable you to live a life worthy of his call. May he give you the power to accomplish all the good things your faith prompts you to do.

2 Thessalonians 3:8-10
8 nor did we eat anyone's food without paying for it. On the contrary, we worked night and day, laboring and

toiling so that we would not be a burden to any of you. [9] We did this, not because we do not have the right to such help, but in order to offer ourselves as a model for you to imitate. 10 For even when we were with you, we gave you this rule: "The one who is unwilling to work shall not eat."

James 4:13-15

[13] Come now, you who say, "Today or tomorrow we will go into such and such a town and spend a year there and trade and make a profit"— [14] yet you do not know what tomorrow will bring. What is your life? For you are a mist that appears for a little time and then vanishes. [15] Instead you ought to say, "If the Lord wills, we will live and do this or that."

# Part Three:

LOCAL MENTORS

MENTORES LOCALES

GID LOKAL

# Best Practices of Local Business Mentors

**Be a Friend:** Show that you're more of a friend than a boss. Spend personal time with them and get to know their families.

**Create a Trusting Environment:** Promise strict confidentiality within Haiti and ask permission to discuss their business with your American mentor. Let mentees know they can expect you to listen with empathy, and provide accountability and support for their work.

**Create Structure Together:** Agree on how often to meet (at least monthly), how long your meetings will be, and where you'll meet. It is important to meet at least some of the time at mentee's place of business. Decide on whether to commit to one or two years.

**Set Goals Together:** Agree on goals for your mentoring relationship, such as growing companies, creating jobs, and helping your community to thrive.

**Encourage Community Service:** Help mentees to use their businesses to serve the community. Start by asking: "What community needs do you care about?" Help them turn their concerns into action, and look for ways you can work together to serve your community.

**Encourage Integrity:** Help mentees build a culture of trust with their employees, customers and suppliers by consistently doing what they promise. Help them build teamwork that leads to win-win relationships.

**Face Challenges Together:** Share how you overcame the same obstacles they're facing, and be honest about the challenges that you still face. Don't pretend to have all the answers – mentees will relate to your weaknesses more than your strengths. Knowing you have struggles will help them face their own.

**Discuss Their Issues**: Allow mentees' current situation to direct the conversation: "What would you like to discuss today?" Ask them early in each mentor visit what opportunities and challenges they're currently facing in their business.

**Ask Thought-Provoking Questions:** Ask questions that help them think through important issues. Discovering the right direction will spur them to change more than being told what to do. (Our Business Health Profile has questions you could ask in each aspect of business leadership.)

**Strategize the Future:** Help mentees shift from just surviving today to creating a thriving future. Affirm their ability to improve their business, help them set long-term goals and work towards them step by step. Show how innovation and determination have improved your business over time.

**Offer Advice:** Each time you meet, offer the one recommendation which will improve their business the most. Share why you think it's important and get their feedback.

**Encourage Goal-Setting:** At the end of each mentor visit, ask them to set and write down one goal to work on until you meet again. Ask how they did on that goal at your next meeting. Show respect for their ideas and affirm their ability to make positive changes.

**Make Connections**: Isolation is one definition of poverty. You're enriched by the connections you have in your community, so a key role of mentors is to connect mentees with people and resources that can add value to their businesses.

**Keep Your Promises:** Write down and follow through on the ways you said you'd help them.

**Keep Your Appointments:** Schedule your next meeting, write it down, and remind them the day before. Be reliable and prompt to build trust and set a good example.

**Ask Them to Mentor Others:** Encourage them to invest in two other entrepreneurs, using the Apostle Paul's words in 2 Timothy 2:2: "And the things you have heard me say in the presence of many witnesses entrust to reliable men who will also be qualified to teach others." Suggest our <u>Locals Mentoring Locals</u> as a simple guide to launch and structure a mentoring relationship.

**Be Positive**: Always find something in their work to compliment. Offer your listening ear, encouragement, prayer and support. Your affirming presence can make a big difference.

**Improve Your Mentoring Skills:** Continue growing as a mentor by reflecting on your mentoring experiences, and learning from reading and interacting with other mentors (both local and international).

# Mejores Prácticas de la Mentoria Empresarial Local

Mejores Prácticas de la Mentoria Empresarial Local

**Sea amigo:** muéstrele que usted es más amigo que jefe. Invierta tiempo personal con ellos y permítase conocer a sus familias.

**Crea un ambiente de confianza:** prometa confidencialidad y pida permiso para discutir algún asunto del negocio con el mentor Norteamericano. Hágale saber que pueden esperar que usted les escuche con empatía, y que provea rendición de cuentas y apoyo para su trabajo.

**Creen una estructura juntos:** pónganse de acuerdo en que tan regularmente se reunirán (por lo menos una vez al mes), que tan largas serán sus reuniones, y donde se van a reunir. Es importante que a veces se reúnan en la empresa del mentoreado. Decida si se comprometerá uno o dos años.

**Pónganse metas juntos:** acuerden que metas alcanzaran en su relación de mentoria, como crecer la compañía, crear empleos, y ayudar a la comunidad a salir adelante.

**Anime al servicio comunitario:** ayude a su mentoreado a usar su empresa para servir a la comunidad. Comience por preguntar, "Que necesidades hay en su comunidad que a usted le interesan?" Ayúdele a transformar sus preocupaciones en acciones, y a encontrar maneras en las que pueden trabajar juntos para servir a la comunidad.

**Anime a la integridad:** ayude a su mentoreado a crear la cultura de confianza en sus empleados, clientes y proveedores consistentemente haciendo lo que prometió que haría. Ayúdele a crear un equipo de trabajo que lleve a relaciones de ganar-ganar.

**Enfrenten riesgos juntos:** comparta como sobresalto los mismos obstáculos que ellos enfrentan, y sea honesto acerca de los retos que aún enfrenta. No pretenda tener respuestas para todo-los mentoreados se relacionaran a sus debilidades más que a sus fortalezas. Saber que usted tiene luchas les ayuda a enfrentar las de ellos.

**Discuta los asuntos de ellos:** permita que la situación de su mentoreado sea lo que le de dirección a la conversación, "Que le gustaría discutir hoy?". Pregúntele anticipadamente en cada visita que oportunidades y retos enfrenta su negocio.

**Haga preguntas que lleven a la reflexión:** haga preguntas que le ayuden a pensar a través de importantes asuntos. Descubrir la dirección correcta provocara el cambio en ellos aún más que si usted simplemente les dice que deben hacer. (Nuestro perfil de estado de empresa tiene preguntas que ustedes pueden hacer).

**Creen estrategias para el futuro:** ayude al mentoreado a cambiar de la mentalidad "de sobrevivir hoy" a crear un futuro brillante. Afírmele en su habilidad para mejorar el negocio, ayúdele a fijar metas a largo-plazo y trabajar hacia ellas paso a paso. Muéstrele como la innovación y la determinación ha mejorado su negocio con el tiempo.

**Ofrezca consejo:** cada vez que se reúna, ofrezca una recomendación que mejorara el negocio. Dígale porque piensa que ese cambio es importante y espere escuchar sus comentarios.

**Anime al establecimiento de metas:** al final de cada visita del mentor, pídale que establezca y escriba una meta en la que puedan trabajar hasta la próxima visita. Pregúntele en la próxima visita como le fue con la meta que se propuso. Muestre respeto a sus ideas y afirme su habilidad de generar cambios positivos.

**Haga conexiones:** el aislarse es definición de pobreza. Usted es enriquecido por las conexiones que posee en su comunidad, así que un rol clave como mentor es que conecte a su mentoreado con otras personas y recursos que puedan añadir valor a su negocio.

**Mantenga sus promesas:** escríbalas y deles seguimiento a las cosas que prometió que haría para ayudar.

**Mantenga sus compromisos:** agenden su próxima reunión, escríbanlo, y luego recuérdense esa fecha un dia antes. Sea confiable y este a tiempo para cultivar confianza y fijar un buen ejemplo.

**Anímeles a ser mentor de otros:** anímeles a invertir en uno o dos empresarios, utilizando lo que dijo el apóstol Pablo en 2 Timoteo 2:2: "Lo que has oído de mi ante muchos testigos, esto encarga a hombres fieles que sean idóneos para enseñar también a otros". Sugiera nuestra guía de <u>Los Locales de Mentoría Locales</u> para estructurar una relación de mentoria.

**Se positive:** siempre encuentre algo en su negocio que usted pueda elogiar. Ofrezca su oído para escuchar, apoyo y oración. Su presencia afirmándole puede simplemente hacer la diferencia.

**Mejore sus habilidades de mentoria:** continúe creciendo como mentor para reflejar en sus experiencias de mentoria, y continué aprendiendo a través de lecturas e interactuando con otros mentores (sea locales o internacionales).

# Pi Bon Pratik Pou Mentor Bizniz Lokal

Tradui pa Dominique Coutard

**Vin yon zanmi**: Montre ke ou plis yon zanmi ke on patwon. Pase ti tan avèk yo epi rankontre fanmi yo.

**Kreye konfyans**: Pwomèt yo ke enfòmasyon sa yo ap rete konfidansyèl, mande yo pèmisyon pou ou pataje enfòmasyon sa yo ak mentor Ameriken ou a. Fòk moun ke w'ap mentore yo konnen ke w'ap tande yo e founi yo bon sipò.

**Kreye yon aranjman ansanm**: Antann nou sou chak kilè n'ap rankontre (pi piti yon fwa pa mwa), kombyen tan rankont yo ap dire e kibo rankont sa yo ap fèt. Li enpòtan pou ou rankontre moun ke w'ap mentore yo nan biznis yo tou.

**Etabli objektif ansanm**: Etabli objektif pou relasyon an, tankou: fè biznis la grandi, ede kominote a pwospere.

**Ankouraje sèvis kominote**: Ede moun ke w'ap mentore yo itilize biznis yo a pou ede kominote a. Fòk yo mande tèt yo "Kisa kominote a bezwen ke yo ka ofri?" Ede yo mete sa ki nan tèt yo an aksyon e jwenn mwayen pou nou travay ansanm pou sèvi kominote a

**Ankouraje entegrite**: Ede moun w'a mentore yo etabli yon konfyans nan anplwaye, kliyan ak founisè ke yo genyen e pou sa fèt, fòk yo kenbe pwomès yo. Ede yo travay an ekip pou yo etabli yon relasyon genyen-genyen.

**Fè fas ak obstak ansanm**: Pataje ak yo mwayen ke ou itilize pou travèse menm obstak ke y'ap travèse a e di yo onètman ki obstak ke w'ap travèse toujou. Pa pretann ke ou gen tout repons yo – moun w'ap mentore yo ap plis atache ak feblès ou ke fòs ou. Si yo konnen ke ou gen obstak tou, sa ap ede yo fe fas ak obstak pa yo.

**Pataje Pwoblèm yo**: Bay moun w'ap mentore yo opòtinite pou yo gide konvesasyon an, oubyen rankont lan. Mande yo "Kisa yo ta renmen diskite jodi a" toujou mande yo ki obstak y'ap konfronte nan moman an anndan bizxnis yo.

**Poze kesyon ki du**: Poze kesyon ki pral ede yo reflechi ak pwoblèm ki enpòtan. Lè yo sou yon bon wout, y'ap plis anvi chanje olye pou yo fè sa yo di yo fè. (Pwofil sante bizxnis nou an gen kesyon ou ka poze sou zafè leadership)

**Strateji pou demen**: Fòk moun w'ap mentore yo soti nan "viv pou jodi" e aprann "viv pou demen". Fòk yo afirme anvi pou yo agrandi bizxnis yo, ede yo etabli objektif pou demen epi travay pou reyalize yo etap pa etap. Montre yo ki inovasyon ak detèminasyon ki ede bizxnis ou a avanse.

**Ba yo konsèy**: Nan chak rankont, ba yo yon konsèy ki ka ede yo amelyore bizxnis yo. Pataje ak yo sa ou panse ki empòtan e tande avi pa yo tou.

**Etabli objektif**: Apre rankont yo, mande yo pou yo ekri yon objektif pou prochen rankont lan. Nan prochen rankont lan, mande yo kòman sa te ye avèk objektif sa.

**Koneksyon**: Separasyon se yon definisyon de povrete. Se koneksyon ou genyen anndan kominote a ki pral anrichi ou, kidonk, travay prensipal yon mentor se konekte moun ke y'ap mentore yo ak resous e moun ki pral bay bizxnis yo plis valè.

**Kenbe pwomès ou**: Ekri fason ke ou te di ou t'ap ede yo et kenbe pwomès sa.

**Onore randevou yo**: Planifye prochen rankont yo, ekri li yon kote e sonje avize yo jou avan an. Fòk ou fyab e rapid pou ou ka kreye konfyans ak bon ekzanp.

**Mande pou yo mentore lòt moun**: Ankouraje yo pou yo envesti nan 2 lòt biznisman menm jan pawòl Paul la di nan 2 Timothee 2:2 "Sa ke mwen di nan prezans anpil temwen konfye ak moun serye ki pral kalifye pou anseye lòt moun" Mande pou bizniman ki

**Rete pozitif**: Toujou jwenn on ti mwayen pou felisite yo pou travay yo. Fè yo konnen ke w'ap tande yo, ankouraje yo, priye pou yo epi sipòte yo. Prezans ou ap fè on gwo diferans.

**Ogmante kapasite mentoring ou**: Eksperyans ou ak sa ou aprann nan enteraksyon ke ou genyen avèk lòt mentor (lokal ak entènasyonal) ap pèmèt ou grandi plis nan wòl mentor a.

# Locals Mentoring Locals

## Establish the Mentoring Relationship:

1. **Find two or three mentees to serve.** Offer to mentor someone with whom you already have mutual respect and trust.

2. **Choose mentees who are open to coaching and whose businesses have strong growth potential.** Make sure they are eager to set and achieve goals, and really committed to growing as leaders and growing their enterprise.

3. **Create a trusting environment.** Promise strict confidentiality. Let mentees know they can expect you to listen with empathy, and provide accountability and support for their work.

4. **Create structure together.** Agree on how often to meet (monthly is a good rhythm), how long your meetings will be, and where you'll meet. (It's important to meet at least some of the time at your mentee's place of business.) Decide on whether to commit to one or two years.

5. **Set goals together.** Agree on expected outcomes of your relationship, such as: revenue growth, job creation, and community service.

6. **Envision them to give back.** Ask if they'd be willing to mentor two others during or after receiving mentorship.

7. **Agree on a format for your meetings.** We recommend the below format.

# Use a Format Like This in Your Monthly Mentoring Sessions:

1. Connect personally, sharing about your families.

2. Ask: "What opportunities and challenges would you like to discuss today?"

3. Discuss their progress on the top two goals they set last month on their GrowBook Action Plan.

4. Discuss a chapter of GrowBook together and apply it to their business.

5. Share insight on their current situation from your own experience.

6. Give your top two recommendations for the coming month and have them choose to goals for the coming month. Both of you record them on the Action Plan.

7. Encourage and pray for them to grow their business, create jobs, and serve their community.

# Know Your Role:

1. **Build relationships.** Making a personal connection is the environment in which the other objectives can flourish. Relationships are where transformation happens, so get acquainted and build trust.

2. **Coach business decisions.** Get to know their business, ask probing questions, and focus attention on aspects of the business where the greatest opportunities and challenges lie. Help them make better decisions and grow the business, leading towards increased revenue and job creation.

3. **Mentor their leadership.** If you focus solely on "coaching

business decisions", you could be accused of giving helpful advice without actually building their own capacity to make wiser decisions and become better business leaders. So, in addition to focusing on the business, focus on the leader of the business. This involves helping them grow personally and professionally in whatever ways will make them better leaders. This could be your most impactful investment.

4. **Make connections.** Isolation is one definition of poverty. We're all incredibly enriched by the connections we have in our community, so one of your key roles as a mentor is to facilitate connections between mentees and the people or resources which could add value to their businesses.

# Los Locales de Mentoría Locales

Traducido por Samuel Hernandez

## Establezca la(s) relación(es) de mentoría:

1. **Encuentre dos o tres personas para mentorear y servirles.** Ofrezca mentorear a alguien con quien usted ya tiene respeto y confianza mutua.

2. **Elija personas a mentorear que estén abiertas a recibir entrenamiento y cuyos negocios tengan un fuerte potencial de crecimiento.** Asegúrese que esas personas estén ansiosas por establecer y cumplir metas, y que estén realmente comprometidas con crecer como líderes y crecer su empresa.

3. **Cree un ambiente de confianza.** Prometa confidencialidad estricta. Haga saber a sus discípulos que pueden esperar que usted escuche con empatía, que asuma responsabilidad por lo que ellos hacen y apoye su trabajo.

4. **Creen estructuras juntos.** Lleguen a acuerdos sobre cada cuánto se reunirán (mensualmente es un buen ritmo), qué tan largas serán sus reuniones, y adónde se reunirán. (Es importante que se reúnan al menos parte de ese tiempo en el negocio de su discípulo.) Decida si se va a comprometer por uno o dos años.

5. **Establecer metas juntos.** Ponerse de acuerdo sobre los resultados esperados de su relación, tales como: crecimiento de los ingresos, la creación de empleo, y el servicio comunitario.

6. **A vislumbrar a devolver.** Pregunte si ellos estarían dispuestos a mentor de otros dos durante o después de recibir la tutoría.

7. **Acordar un formato para sus reuniones.** Le recomendamos el siguiente formato.

## Formato para Reuniones Mensuales de Tutoría:

1. Conecte personalmente, compartan sobre sus familias.

2. Pregunte: "¿Que oportunidades y que retos quiere descurtir hoy?"

3. Analice su progreso en las dos primeras metas que se fijan el mes pasado en su GrowBook Plan de Acción.

4. Discuta un capítulo de GrowBook juntos y aplicarlo a su negocio.

5. Compartir una visión sobre la situación actual de su propia experiencia.

6. Dé a sus dos mejores recomendaciones para el próximo mes y hacer que se eligen a los objetivos para el próximo mes. Ambos grabarlas en el Plan de Acción.Hablen sobre el progreso de las dos recomendaciones más importantes que fueron discutidas en la última reunión.

7. Anime y ore para que el negocios crezca, que el negocio crea trabajos, y que puedan ser siervos a la comunidad.

## Conozca su rol:

1. **Construya relaciones.** La creación de una conexión personal es el ambiente en el cual los demás objetivos pueden florecer. Las relaciones son el lugar donde sucede la transformación, así que familiarícese y construya confianza.

2. **Asesore decisiones de negocio.** Conozca el negocio de sus

discípulos, haga preguntas y concentre su atención en los aspectos del negocio donde se encuentran las más grandes oportunidades y desafíos. Ayúdeles a tomar mejores decisiones y a crecer su negocio, llevándolos a incrementar sus ingresos y crear empleos.

3. **Mentoree su liderazgo.** Si se enfoca solamente en "mentorear decisiones de negocios", usted podría ser acusado de dar consejo útil sin realmente construir su capacidad de tomar decisiones más sabias y ser mejores líderes de negocio. Así que, además de concentrarse en el negocio, concéntrese en el líder del negocio. Esto implica ayudarles a crecer personal y profesionalmente en cualquier manera que les haga mejores líderes. Ésta puede ser su inversión con mayor impacto.

4. **Haga conexiones.** El aislamiento es una definición de pobreza. Somos increíblemente enriquecidos por las conexiones que tenemos en nuestra comunidad, así que uno de nuestros roles principales como mentores es facilitar las conexiones entre nuestros discípulos y las personas o recursos que podrían agregar valor a su negocio.

# Ayisyen k'ap ankadre Biznismann

Tradui pa Colibri Translation Services

## Etabli relasyon gid-disip la (yo):

1. **Chache de ou twa disip ou kapab sèvi.** Ofri sèvis gid bay yon moun ou deja respekte e fè konfyans e ki deja gen yon respè ak yon konfyans pou ou.

2. **Chwazi disip ki reseptif a fòmasyon ou e ki posede biznis ki gen anpil potansyèl pou grandi.** Asire ke yo motive pou fikse e acheve objektif, e ke yo pral angaje tèt yo antan ke lidè pou yo grandi e grandi biznis yo.

3. **Kreye yon anviwònman de konfyans.** Pwomèt yo ke w pap pataje okenn ti detay yo ba w ak pèsonn lòt moun. Fè disip la konprann ke li kapab atann ou koute li ak konpasyon e ba li redevabilite ak sipò nan travay li.

4. **Kreye yon pwogram ansanm.** Deside chak ki lè nou pral reyini (chak mwa kapab yon bon rit), ki longè reyinyon nou yo pral genyen, e ki kote nou pral reyini. (Li enpòtan pou reyini o mwens de tanzantan nan biznis moun wap gide a.) Deside si nou pral angaje nou pou en an ou dezan.

5. Fikse bi ansanm. Mwen dakò sou rezilta atann de relasyon ou, tankou: revni grandi, kreyasyon travay, ak sèvis nan kominote a.

6. Anvizaje yo bay tounen. Mande yo si yo ta kapab byen vle konseye de lòt moun pandan oswa apre li fin resevwa gid.

7. Mwen dakò sou yon fòma pou reyinyon ou yo. Nou rekòmande fòma ki anba a.

## Fòma Rankont Pou Sesyon
## Mentora Chak Mwa:

1. Koneksyon pèsonèl, pataje enfòmasyon sou fanmi ou.

2. Chèche konnen "Ki opòtinite ak defi ke ou ta renmen diskite jodi a?"

3. Diskite pwogrè yo sou de objektif yo tèt mwa pase a sou Sèptanm Yo GrowBook Plan Aksyon yo.

4. Diskite yon chapit nan GrowBook ansanm ak aplike li nan biznis yo.

5. Pataje opinyon ou sou sitiyasyon aktyèl yo a pati de eksperyans ou.

6. Bay de Rekòmandasyon tèt ou pou mwa a ap vini epi fè yo chwazi objektif pou mwa kap vini an. Tou de nan nou dosye yo sou Plan an Aksyon.

7. Ankouraje yo e priye pou kwasans biznis yo, pou yo kreye job e sèvi kominote a.

## Konnen kisa wòl ou ye:

1. **Bati relasyon.** Lè w fè yon koneksyon pèsonèl, sa kreye yon anviwònman kote lòt objektif ou yo kapab reyisi. Transfòmasyon fèt nan relasyon, donk ou bezwen fè konesans lòt moun nan e enspire konfyans nan li.

2. **Konseye yo nan desizyon biznis.** Abitye w ak biznis yo, poze yo kesyon ki gen fòs, epi konsantre atansyon w sou aspè biznis la kote gen pi gran opòtinite ak pi gran defi. Ede yo pran pi

bon desizyon pou grandi biznis la, bagay ki pral pèmèt yo fè plis lajan e kreye plis anplwa.

3. **Antrene lidè yo.** Si w konsantre w sèlman sou « konseye yo nan desizyon biznis yo », gen yon danje ke wap bay konsèy itil san w pa grandi kapasite yo pou yo pran desizyon ki pi saj pou tèt pa yo e devni pi bon lidè nan biznis. Pa fokalize sou biznis la sèlman, fokalize sou lidè biznis la. Sa vle di ede yo grandi pèsonèlman e pwofesyonèlman nan nenpòt ki fason kap rann yo pi bon lidè. Li posib ke se envestisman sa a kap bay pi bon rannman.

4. **Kreye lyen.** Yon definisyon pou mo povrete a se izolasyon. Nou tout nou jwenn anpil benefis ak richès nan lyen nou genyen ak lòt moun nan komin nou yo. Se sak fè yonn nan wòl ou yo kòm yon gid ki kle se pou fasilite koneksyon ant moun yo wap antrene ak moun oubyen resous ki kapab ajoute valè pou biznis yo.

# Local Mentor Program

This is an attempt to design a process for successfully launching and sustaining a local mentoring program, based on the conviction that the most sustainable way to multiply our efforts is to see local entrepreneurs taking up the mentoring mantle and effectively helping their fellow entrepreneurs to grow companies, create jobs, and help their communities thrive.

## Recruit/Envision

1. Identify strong candidates with the necessary skills, experience, attitudes, and maturity. Invite them to interest meetings and explain the program well.

2. Share advantages of local vs. international mentorship: no barriers of distance, culture, or language.

3. Envision them to see business as a calling that serves the world.

4. Share the biblical basis and mandate to invest in others.

5. Explain how local mentorship is strategic for impacting their own country by growing companies, creating jobs, and helping communities to thrive.

6. Share the principle that effective change comes from within a community, citing p.206 of Lawrence Harrison's <u>Central Liberal Truth</u>: "Progress endures only when it is driven chiefly from within."

7. Help prepare mentees to become mentors, by involving them in quarterly peer mentoring sessions which will build their coaching experience.

8.  Provide several small steps for candidates to move towards becoming a local mentor, understanding that such a large and unfamiliar commitment will take time to embrace. One such small step could be to join international mentors on their mentoring sessions. Getting a chance to try it is the best way to build vision, excitement and skills for mentoring.

# Orient/Train

1.  Explain the qualifications, especially having started and grown a profitable business as well as exhibiting an attitude of servanthood.

2.  Explain the role, including:

    a.  developing entrepreneurs as leaders

    b.  building capacity of the entrepreneurs to make good decisions by using questions to help them discover solutions to their own challenges

    c.  coaching entrepreneurs towards business efficiency and growth

    d.  coaching entrepreneurs to use their businesses to help their communities thrive

    e.  connect entrepreneurs to people, resources, and capital (if possible) to help them grow

3.  Stress the importance of building a trusting personal relationship through consistent presence, listening, encouragement, prayer, and accountability.

4.  Explain the scheduled commitments:

    a.  Orientation and training events

    b.  Mentoring sessions (monthly, or at least quarterly)

    c.   Meet regularly with other local mentors

    d.   Two year term

5. Encourage proactive scheduling of the mentoring sessions, confirming the day before, and being on time.

6. Set expectation that mentees will set the agenda for mentoring sessions. Mentors should ask at the outset: "What areas of your leadership and business would you like our discussions to focus on? Towards the beginning of each session, mentors should ask: "What would you like to discuss today?"

7. Train mentors in use of GrowBook, encouraging them to read and apply with mentees one chapter each month.

## Match Mentors to Mentees:

1. Have both mentors and mentees fill out the GrowBook Action Plan, then look for mentor strengths that match mentee weaknesses.

2. Whenever possible, look for complementary personalities.

3. Look for similar industries and nearby locations.

4. Schedule separate meetings with two different potential mentors, and ask mentee which one could teach him/her more.

5. In addition to providing mentees from within the program, encourage mentors to begin mentoring entrepreneurs they already have trusting relationships with.

6. If you provide a more than one mentor for each mentee, limit it to two mentors, with one being the "lead mentor" and the other being the "support mentor".

# Ongoing Support

1. International mentors provide quarterly training to local mentors: coaching their coaching skills, discussing the entrepreneurs and businesses they serve. In these meetings, discuss the challenges and opportunities in the local mentor's own business as well, perhaps using one third of the time on this.

2. Local mentors should meet with each other monthly for ongoing support and encouragement.

3. An annual local mentor training retreat can accelerate vision and skills of new and ongoing local mentors.

# Life Cycle of our International Programs

1. Year 1-2: Four trips per year – Mentoring and training entrepreneurs through GrowBook while grooming potential local mentors and raising capacity of local organization to oversee a local mentoring program.

2. Year 3: Three trips per year – Mentoring alongside local mentors, passing on leadership to them.

3. Year 4 onward: Two trips per year – Maintaining relationships with local mentors and helping them multiply mentors.

# Barriers to Building a Strong Local Mentor Program

4. Lack of community in the group of entrepreneurs.

5. Culture of mistrust in the wider business community.

6. Lack of culture of mentoring.

7. Overly lofty expectations of what it takes to be a mentor (expected to have all the answers rather than offering support and encouragement as well as some advice).

8. Lack of self-confidence in one's own abilities and experience.

9. Perception that Americans are exclusively qualified as business mentors.

10. Difficulty setting and keeping regular appointments.

11. Lack of coordination by a local point person.

# Questions

1. How and how often should local mentors connect with international mentors concerning the entrepreneurs they co-mentor?

2. If enough local mentors are found, is there any reason not to assign them to entrepreneurs not receiving international mentorship?

3. Must local mentoring relationships always be gender specific?

4. Are two mentees per mentor an ideal ratio?

5. What is the best process for matching mentors to mentees?

6. How can we help mentor/mentee relationships get off to a strong start?

# Additional Resources to
# Empower Local Mentors

1. Entrepreneur Application for a Mentor, by LEAD

2. Boss vs. Mentor, from article entitled "Coaching" by Dr. Allison Rossett

3. What Good Mentors Do, from article entitled "The Art of Coaching" by Vistage

4. Biblical Basis for Mentoring, in the Partners Worldwide Mentoring Handbook

5. Mentoring Agreement Template, in the Partners Worldwide Mentoring Handbook

# Programa de Tutores Locales

Traducido por Samuel Hernandez

Esto es un atento para diseñar un proceso para iniciar y sostener un programa de tutores locales basado en la convicción que la forma más sostenible para multiplicar nuestros esfuerzos es que veamos empresarios locales tomando el manto de tutor y asimismo pueden ayudar efectivamente a sus compatriota empresarios a crecer compañías, crear trabajos, y ayudar a sus comunidades a prospera.

## Reclutar / Imaginar

1. Identifique talentos, experiencias, actitudes, y madurez que los cualifica para ser tutores a empresarios.

2. Comparta las ventajas de tutores locales contra uno internacional. No hay barreras de distancia, cultura, o lenguaje.

3. Llévelos a que imaginen negocios como un llamado para servir al mundo.

4. Comparta la base bíblica y el mandato de impartir sabiduría y conocimiento en otros.

5. Explique cómo tutores locales es estratégico para impactar a su propio país, atreves del crecimiento de compañías, creando trabajos y ayudando a comunidades prosperar.

6. Comparta el principio que dice que cambio efectivo viene de adentro de una comunidad, citando p. 206 de Lawerence Harrison's "Central Liberal Truth"; "El progreso permanece solamente cuando viene primeramente de adentro."

7. Identifique candidatos fuertes e invítelos a reuniones de interés que enfoquen en los objetivos mencionados anteriormente y explique el programa bien.

8. Ayude preparar aprendiz a ser tutores, involucrándolos en sesiones tutoriales de compatriotas cada trimestre. Esto les ayudara su experiencia como tutor.

9. Provea unos cuantos pasos pequeños para que candidatos se puedan mover más cerca a hacer tutores locales.

## Oriente / Guie

1. Explique las cualificaciones, especialmente la de haber empezado y crecido un negocio lucrativo, igual que exhibiendo una actitud de sirviente.

2. Explique la funciones, incluyendo:

   a. Desarrollo empresario como lideres

   b. Creciendo las capacidades del empresario para hacer buenas decisiones usando preguntas para ayudarlos descubrir soluciones a sus propios retos.

   c. Prepare a los empresarios hacia el crecimiento y eficiencia del negocio o empresa.

   d. Prepare a los empresarios a que usen negocios para ayudar a que la comunidad prospere.

   e. Conecté a empresarios a gente, recursos, y capital (cuando posible) para ayudarlos a crecer.

3. Deje conocer la importancia de crear una relación personal en pura confianza, a través de su presencia constante, escuchando a su aprendiz, animándolo, orando por el aprendiz y contabilidad del aprendiz.

4. Explique los compromiso programados:

    a. Orientación y eventos de entrenamientos

    b. Sesiones de tutoría trimestral

    c. Llamadas de teléfono a los aprendices cada tres meses

    d. Reúnase dos veces al año con otros tutores locales

    e. Reúnase dos veces al año con otros tutores internacionales

    f. Un periodo de dos años

5. Anime planificación proactiva para las sesiones de tutoriales, confirme el día antes, y llegue a tiempo.

6. Tenga expectaciones que aprendices establecerán la agenda para la sesiones tutoriales. Mentores deben preguntar desde el principio: "¿Qué área de liderazgo y negocios ellos quieren enfocar las discusiones hoy?" Al principio de cada sesión, el tutor debe preguntar: "¿De qué quiere hablar hoy?"

7. Entrene tutores a usar el "El Perfil de la Salude del Negocio" (1. Business Health Profile) incluyendo:

    a. La arte de la pregunta

    b. Como usarla en una sesión de tutorial

    c. Como usarla para aprender sobre el negocio y el progreso del registro

    d. La importancia de usarla para registrar recomendaciones para el tutor y el aprendiz.

    e. La importancia de rápidamente poniendo al día y entregándosela a el aprendiz después de cada sesión

# Los mentores de partido para aprendices:

1. Tener ambos mentores y aprendices completan el GrowBook Plan de Acción, entonces buscan fortalezas mentores que responden a debilidades aprendiz.

2. Siempre que sea posible, busque personalidades complementarias.

3. Busque industrias similares y otras regiones.

4. Programe reuniones por separado con dos mentores potenciales diferentes, y pedir aprendiz cuál podía enseñarle / ella más.

5. Además de proporcionar aprendices desde el programa, alentar mentores para comenzar la tutoría empresarios que ya tienen relaciones de confianza con.

6. Si usted proporciona un más que un mentor para cada aprendiz, limitarlo a dos mentores, uno de los cuales el "mentor de plomo" y el otro es el "apoyo mentora".

# Apoyo continuo

1. Los mentores internacionales brindan capacitación trimestral a los mentores locales: entrenar sus habilidades de coaching, la discusión de los empresarios y las empresas a las que sirven. En estas reuniones, discutir los retos y oportunidades en la propia empresa del mentor local, así, tal vez usando una tercera parte del tiempo en esto.

2. Los mentores locales deben cumplir con los demás mensual de apoyo y estímulo.

3. Un retiro anual de formación mentora local puede acelerar la visión y habilidades de los nuevos y actuales mentores locales.

# Ciclo de vida de nuestros programas internacionales

1. Año 1-2: Cuatro viajes al año - Mentoring y entrenar a los empresarios a través GrowBook mientras que la preparación potenciales mentores locales y el aumento de la capacidad de organización local para supervisar un programa de tutoría local.

2. Año 3: Tres viajes al año - Mentoring junto mentores locales, pasando sobre el liderazgo a ellos.

3. Año 4 en adelante: dos viajes por año - Mantener relaciones con los mentores locales y ayudarles multiplican mentores.

# Barreras Que Hay Cuando Creciendo un Programa de Tutores Locales

1. Falta de una comunidad en el grupo de empresarios

2. Una cultura de desconfianza entre la comunidad de negocios en general

3. Falta de una cultura de tutores

4. Expectaciones elevadas sobre que toma ser un tutor (Esperan que tengan todas las contestaciones en vez de ofrecer soporte y animar igual que un poco de concejo)

5. Falta de confianza propia en sus habilidades y experiencias

6. La percepción que solo los norte americanos son cualificados para ser tutores de negocios

7. Dificultad en estableciendo y manteniendo citas regulares

8. Falta de coordinación por una persona local

# Preguntas

1. ¿Cómo y cuantas veces deben tutores locales conectar con los tutores internacionales sobre empresarios que ellos tutoran juntos?

2. ¿Deben los tutores locales e internacionales actualizar El Perfil de la Salude del Negocio de empresarios que tutoran juntos?

3. ¿Si hay suficiente tutores, hay alguna razone por la cual no se debe asignarlos a empresarios que no están siendo tutorados por internacionales?

4. ¿Deben relaciones de tutores locales tener en cuenta el sexo del empresario?

5. ¿Son dos aprendices por tutor la proporción ideal?

6. ¿Cuál es el mejor proceso para juntar aprendiz a tutor?

7. ¿Cómo podemos ayudar relaciones entre el tutor y el aprendiz empezar de buena forma?

# Recursos adicionales para Empower mentores locales

1. Entrepreneur Application for a Mentor, by LEAD

2. Boss vs. Mentor, from article entitled "Coaching" by Dr. Allison Rossett

3. What Good Mentors Do, from article entitled "The Art of Coaching" by Vistage

4. Biblical Basis for Mentoring, in the Partners Worldwide Mentoring Handbook

5. Mentoring Agreement Template, in the Partners Worldwide Mentoring Handbook

# Pwogram pou Gid Lokal

Tradui pa Colibri Translation Services

Sa se yon efò pou devlope yon pwosesis pou lanse e mentni yon pwogram pou gid lokal ki va reyisi. Pwogram sa a baze sou yon konviksyon ki di ke fason ki pi dirab ke nou kapab miltipliye efò nou yo se pou antreprenè lokal pran rèskonsabilite pou sèvi tankou gid biznis pou ede antreprenè parèy yo grandi konpayi yo, kreye anplwa, e ede kominote yo fleri.

## Rekrite/Anvizyone

1. Idantifye kèk kandida fò ki genyen konpetans, eksperyans, atitid, ak matirite ki nesesè. Envite yo nan yon reyinyon e byen esplike pwogram la ba yo.

2. Pataje avantaj yon pwogram gid lokal genyen parapò a yon pwogram entènasyonal: nan pwen baryè distans, kilti, ou lang.

3. Ba yo vizyon an: biznis se yon vokasyon ki pèmèt yon moun sèvi monn nan.

4. Pataje baz biblik la ak rèskonsabilite nou genyen pou envesti nan lòt moun.

5. Esplike yo ki jan yon pwogram gid lokal se yon bagay ki stratejik pou fè yon enpak nan peyi yo e pou grandi konpayi yo, kreye anplwa, e ede kominote yo fleri.

6. Pataje prensip la ki di ke chanjman efikas toujou soti andedan yon kominote, tankou li ekri sou paj 206 nan liv Lawrence Harrison, <u>La Vérité Libérale Centrale</u>: « Pwogrè pa janm dire si se pa moun ki anndan kominote a ki lakòz pwogrè a ».

7. Prepare disip pou tounen gid. Yon fason w kapab fè sa se pou w envite yo chak trimès nan yon sesyon fòmasyon pou gid. Sa va ede yo paske lap ba yo plis eksperyans nan fòme lòt moun.

8. Bay kandida w yo plizyè ti etap yo kapab pran pou fè pwogrè anvan yo tounen yon gid lokal. Se pou w pasyan ak yo, paske se yon gwo angajman yap pran e yo pa fin abitye ak pwosesis la. Sa ka mande yo kèk tan anvan yo fin dakò pran angajman sa a. Yon etap ou kapab ba yo se pou yo reyini ak gid entènasyonal yo nan sesyon fòmasyon an. Si w bay yo yon chans pou eksperimante pwosesis la yo menm anvan yo eseye fòme lòt moun, sa se pi bon fason pou kreye vizyon, antisipasyon, ak konpetans nan nouvo gid.

# Oryante/Fòme

1. Esplike kalifikasyon yo ba yo, sitou kalifikasyon an ki di se pou yo te lanse e devlope yon biznis kap fè pwofi deja ak sila ki di se pou yo gen yon kè pou sèvi lòt moun.

2. Esplike yo wòl gid la, ki gen ladan li:

    a. devlope antreprenè kòm lidè

    b. grandi kapasite antreprenè genyen pou pran bon desizyon nan poze yo keksyon ki va pouse yo dekouvri solisyon yo pou pwòp defi pa yo

    c. fòme antreprenè pou yo pi efikas e pou yo grandi biznis yo

    d. fòme antreprenè pou yo sèvi ak biznis yo pou ede kominote yo fleri

    e. konekte antreprenè yo ak moun, resous, e kapital (si sa posib) pou ede yo grandi

3. Strese konbyen sa enpòtan pou yo toujou prezan pou disip

la, pou yo koute li, ankouraje li, priye pou li, e kenbe li reskonsab. Tout bagay sa yo va ede yo bati yon relasyon pèsonèl de konfyans ak disip la.

4. Esplike yo angajman yo bezwen pran nan pwogram yo:

   a. Evènman oryantasyon ak fòmasyon

   b. Sesyon gid-disip (chak mwa, ou o mwens chak trimès)

   c. Reyinyon regilye ak lòt gid lokal

   d. Angajman pou de (2) ane

5. Ankouraje yo pou yo pran devan nan pwogramasyon reyinyon gid-disip yo. Se pou yo konfime reyinyon an ak disip la yon jou anvan yo gen pou yo reyini e se pou yo rive a lè.

6. Kominike yo ke se disip la ki pou detèmine kisa yo pral pale pandan sesyon gid-disip yo. Nan debi reyinyon an, se pou gid yo poze keksyon sa: « Sou ki domèn nan lidèchip ak biznis ou ou ta renmen pale jodi a? » Nan debi chak sesyon, gid la ta dwe mande: « Sou kisa w ta renmen pale jodi a? »

7. Fòme gid yo pou yo sèvi ak GrowBook. Ankouraje yo pou yo li li e pou yo mete yon chapit an pratik ak disip yo chak mwa.

## Jwenn Gid ak Disip:

1. Fè ni gid yo ni disip yo ranpli Plan Daksyon GrowBook la, epi chache jwenn gid ak disip ki fèb menm kote yo fò.

2. Nenpòt lè sa posib, chache moun ki gen pèsonalite konplemantè.

3. Eseye mete moun kap travay nan sektè similè e ki viv pre yonn ak lòt ansanm.

4. Pwograme de (2) reyinyon pou disip la ak de gid diferan, epi kite disip deside nan men kilès li kapab aprann plis.

5. Gid pa oblije sèlman fòme disip kap patisipe nan pwogram lan. Ankouraje yo pou yo konmanse fòme disip ke yo deja konnen e ki fè yo konfyans deja.

6. Si w chwazi bay chak disip plis ke yon sèl gid, pa ba yo plis ke de, e deziye yonn nan yo « gid prensipal » e lòt la « gid de soutyen ».

## Sipò Kontini

1. Gid entènasyonal fòme gid lokal chak trimès: yo fòme yo nan konpetans pou fòmasyon yo, e yo pale ak yo sou antreprenè ak biznis yo ke yap sèvi. Nan reyinyon sa yo, se pou nou pale sou defi ak opòtinite yo ke gid lokal la wè nan biznis li tou. Sa ta dwe okipe yon tyè konsa nan tan reyinyon an.

2. Se pou gid lokal yo reyini yonn ak lòt chak mwa pou yo kapab kontinye sipòte e ankouraje yonn ak lòt.

3. Yon konferans ànyèl pou gid lokal yo kapab akselere vizyon ak konpetans gid lokal yo—ni sa yo ki la lontan, ni sa yo ki apèn konmanse.

## Sik de Vi Pwogram Entènasyonal Nou An

1. 1e, 2e Ane: Kat vwayaj pa ane – Nou gide e fòme antreprenè atravè GrowBook pandan nap prepare moun ki gen potansyèl pou devni gid lokal e nou grandi kapasite yon òganizasyon lokal pou dirije yon pwogram gid lokal.

2. 3e Ane: Twa vwayaj pa ane – Nou sèvi tankou gid en patenarya ak gid lokal yo, e nou transmèt rèskonsabilite nou yo ba yo.

3. 4e Ane e aprè: De vwayaj pa ane – Nou mentni relasyon nou ak gid lokal yo e nou ede yo devlope plis gid.

## Obstak ki Anpeche Moun Devlope yon Pwogram pou Gid Lekòl ki Efikas

4. Si pa gen tèt ansanm nan gwoup antreprenè a.

5. Si antreprenè yo nan kominote a pa fè yonn ak lòt konfyans.

6. Si moun nan kilti a pa gen yon ide de sa sa vle di pou sèvi tankou yon gid pou lòt moun.

7. Si moun ap tann twòp nan men gid (pa egzanp, si yo kwè gid la ta dwe genyen tout repons yo olye pou li ta sèlman ofri sipò ak ankourajman ak kèk bon konsèy).

8. Si moun manke gen konfyans nan pwòp kapasite ak eksperyans yo.

9. Si moun kwè ke se blan sèlman ki kalifye pou sèvi tankou gid biznis.

10. Si moun jwenn sa difisil pou fikse e pou kenbe randevou regilye.

11. Si pa gen yon moun lokal kap kowòdone gid ak disip.

## Keksyon

1. Kòman e chak ki lè gid lokal ta dwe konekte ak gid entènasyonal konsènan antreprenè yo ke yap fòme ansanm?

2. Si nou kapab jwenn ase gid lokal, èske gen yon rezon poukisa nou pa ta dwe mete yo ansanm ak antreprenè ki pa gen gid entènasyonal?

3. Eske nou ta dwe sèlman mete gason ak gason, fi ak fi?

4. Eske de disip pou chak gid se yon rapò ideyal?

5. Kisa ki pi bon fason pou mete gid ansanm ak disip?

6. Kòman nou kapab ede relasyon gid/disip yo kòmanse byen?

## Lòt Resous pou Ekipe Gid Lokal

7. Entrepreneur Application for a Mentor (Aplikasyon Antreprenè pou Jwenn yon Gid), pa LEAD

8. Boss vs. Mentor (Yon Patron Konpare ak yon Gid), ki soti nan atik la ki entitile "Coaching" (Antrènman) pa Dr. Allison Rossett

9. What Good Mentors Do (Sa Bon Gid Fè), ki soti nan atik la ki entitile "The Art of Coaching" (La de Lantrènman) pa Vistage

10. Biblical Basis for Mentoring (Baz Biblik pou Pwosesis Gid La), ki twouve nan Partners Worldwide Mentoring Handbook

11. Mentoring Agreement Template (Modèl pou Yon Akò pou Pwosesis Gid La), ki twouve nan Partners Worldwide Mentoring Handbook

# Local Mentor Application

## Local Mentor Qualifications:

1. Read GrowBook.

2. Demonstrate expertise in at least three of GrowBook's 25 growth drivers.

3. Follow good bookkeeping practices.

4. Run a profitable business.

5. Exhibit an attitude of servanthood.


## Local Mentor Requirements:

1. Commit to visiting your mentee's business(es) monthly for one year.

2. Regularly listen to, pray for, encourage, and coach your mentee(s).

3. Discuss a chapter of GrowBook each month with your mentee(s), helping mentee(s) make application in their own business(es).

4. Receive quarterly training for mentors.

5. Meet monthly (or at least quarterly) with fellow local mentors for mutual support and accountability.

6. Regularly communicate with international mentors about any mentees you co-mentor with them.

# Local Mentor Application:

1. Please comment on how you meet the above "Qualifications".

2. Please comment on your ability and willingness to meet the above "Requirements".

3. What areas of expertise in business would you like to share with your mentee? Refer to the GrowBook Action Plan.

4. Describe the current health and profitability of your own business?

5. Why are you interested in becoming a local mentor?

# Aplicación para Mentor Local

Traducido por Cross Lingo

## Calificaciones para un Mentor Local:

1. Leer el GrowBook

2. Demostrar experiencia en al menos tres de las 25 claves de crecimiento del GrowBook

3. Seguir buenas prácticas de registro contable

4. Operar un negocio rentable

5. Exhibir una actitud de servicio

## Requisitos para un Mentor Local:

1. Comprometerse a visitar mensualmente durante un año el negocio (s) a los cuales él está dando la mentoría

2. Escuchar a, orar por, motivar y capacitar a sus aprendices con regularidad

3. Discutir un capítulo del GrowBook cada mes con su aprendiz(ces), ayudándole a aplicarlo en su propio negocio(s).

4. Recibir trimestralmente entrenamiento para mentores.

5. Reunirse mensualmente (o al menos trimestralmente) con sus compañeros de mentoría local para apoyo mutuo y rendición de cuentas.

6. Comunicarse con regularidad con los mentores internacionales

para conversar acerca de cualquier aprendiz que usted co-mentoreé con ellos

## Aplicación para Mentor Local:

1. Por favor comente sobre cómo usted cumple con las "Calificaciones" detalladas anteriormente.

2. Por favor comente sobre su habilidad y deseo de cumplir con los "Requisitos" detallados anteriormente.

3. ¿Qué áreas de experiencia en los negocios le gustaría compartir con su aprendiz? Vea el Plan de Acción del GrowBook.

4. Describa la salud y rentabilidad actual de su propio negocio.

5. ¿Por qué está interesado en convertirse en un mentor local?

# Aplikasyon pou Gid Lokal

Tradui pa Colibri Translation Services

## Kalifikasyon pou Gid Lokal:

1. Li GrowBook.

2. Montre ke w gen bon konprann nan o mwens twa nan 25 katalizè devlopman yo ki kouvri nan GrowBook.

3. Sèvi ak bon pratik nan kontabilite w.

4. Opere yon biznis k'ap fè pwofi.

5. Montre ke w gen yon kè pou sèvi lòt moun.

## Egzijans pou Gid Lokal:

1. Angaje w pou w rann chak nan biznis disip ou yo yon vizit chak mwa pandan en an.

2. Pale ak disip ou yo souvan. Koute yo, priye pou yo, ankouraje yo, e fòme yo.

3. Pale sou yon chapit nan GrowBook chak mwa ak disip ou (yo). Ede disip ou (yo) mete sa y'ap aprann an pratik nan pwòp biznis pa yo.

4. Resevwa fòmasyon pou gid chak trimès.

5. Reyini chak mwa (ou o mwens chak trimès) ak lòt gid parèy ou yo pou nou kapab sipòte yonn ak lòt e rann kont yonn bay lòt.

6. Kenbe kontak regilye ak gid entènasyonal yo o sijè de nenpòt disip nap gide ansanm.

## Aplikasyon pou Gid Lokal:

1. Esplike pou nou, silvouplè, ki jan ou reponn a tout "Kalifikasyon" yo ki ekri anwo.

2. Dekri pou nou, silvouplè, ki kapasite ak volonte w genyen pou reponn a "Egzijans" yo ki ekri anwo.

3. Nan ki domèn eske w gen anpil konesans ke w ta renmen pataje ak disip ou? Ou kapab li Plan Daksyon GrowBook la pou wè kèk egzanp.

4. Pale nou de sante finansyè biznis ou a genyen aktyèlman.

5. Poukisa w vle sèvi tankou yon gid biznis lokal?

# Local Mentor Panel Discussion

## Questions for Mentors and Mentees:

1. How did your mentoring relationship start?

2. How often do you meet and what do you do in your meetings?

3. What does it take to be a good mentor?

## Questions for Mentees:

1. How does your mentor support you without telling you what to do?

2. Even though you value your mentor's experience and advice, how does he show you that he's a friend and not above you?

3. What do you appreciate about having a Haitian as a mentor?

## Questions for Mentors:

1. What have you gained from being a mentor?

2. What is the hardest part of being a mentor?

3. Why are you helping your competitors?

## Questions for Audience:

1. Do you think we should encourage more local mentorship?

2. How many of you would be willing to either give or receive mentorship?

3.  What can we do to overcome the following barriers to building a strong local mentor program?

    • Lack of regular meeting of entrepreneurs for mutual support.

    • Culture of mistrust in the wider business community.

    • Lack of culture of mentoring.

    • Overly lofty expectations of what it takes to be a mentor (expected to have all the answers rather than offering support and encouragement as well as some advice).

    • Lack of self-confidence in one's own abilities and experience.

    • Perception that Americans are exclusively qualified as business mentors.

    • Difficulty setting and keeping regular appointments.

    • Lack of coordination by a local point person.

# Deba pou Mentor Local

Tradui pa Dominique Coutard

## Kesyon pou mentor ak moun k'ap resevwa mentora yo

1. Kijan relasyon mentor a kòmanse?

2. Chak ki lè nou rankontre e kisa nou fè nan rankont yo?

3. Kisa sa mande pou vin yon bon mentor?

## Kesyon pou moun k'ap resevwa mentora yo

1. Kijan ke mentor a sipòte ou san ke li pa di ou kisa pou ou fè.

2. Menm si ou valorize eksperyans ak konsèy mentor a, kòman li montre ou ke li pa yon patwon ki sou tèt ou, men ki sa yon zanmi?

3. Di kisa ou renmen dèske ou genyen yon Ayisyen kòm mentor.

## Kesyon pou mentor:

1. Kisa travay mentor a rapote w'?

2. Kisa ki pi difisil nan fe travay mentor

3. Poukisa ou deside ede konpetitè ou yo?

## Kesyon pou asistans:

1.  Eske ou panse nou ta sipoze ankouraje plis mentor local?

2.  Konbyen nan nou ki dako vin yo mentor oubyen resevwa èd yon mentor?

3.  Kisa nou ka fè pou nou elimine pwoblèm sa yo ki anpeche nou fè travay mentor local la bien?

    *   Pa gen ase rankont pou sipòte youn lòt.

    *   Pa gen konfyans nan kominote a

    *   Nou pa abitye ak system mentor a.

    *   Nou atann nou a jwenn tout repons olye ke nou resevwa sipò ak ankourajman sèlman

    *   Nou pa kwe nan kapasite nou ak eksperyans nou

    *   Nou deja mete nan tèt nou ke Ameriken deja kalifye pou fè travay sa.

    *   Difikilte pou nou òganize yon rankont

    *   Pa gen koòdinayson

# Part Four:

INTERNATIONAL LEAD MENTORS

MENTORES PLOMO INTERNACIONALES

GID PRENSIPAL ENTÈNASYONAL

# Job Description of Lead Mentors:

1. Work with partner organization(s) to select 9-12 qualified recipient entrepreneurs and replace those who dropout or lose their capacity and/or motivation to grow their businesses.

2. Work effectively with in-country coordinator/translator.

3. Lead quarterly Mentor Visits and update each entrepreneur's GrowBook Action Plan afterwards.

4. Recruit and orient a team of quality mentors to serve on Mentor Visits.

5. Help fellow mentors use their gifts and have a positive experience.

6. Use GrowBook to teach group and individual seminars and encourage its year round use so that training compliments the mentoring process.

7. Encourage entrepreneurs to meet with each other to encourage, support, pray and do business together.

8. Develop local mentors by envisioning top performers, taking them with you to mentoring sessions and training them with "Best Practices of International Mentors".

9. Commit to the role for 2 years.

10. Advance Creating Jobs Inc's vision and mission, in keeping with its values.

# 10 Qualities of International Lead Mentors:

1. Passionate about Creating Jobs Inc's vision and mission, and aligned with its values.

2. Willing and able to lead quarterly Mentor Visits and write follow up reports on each business.

3. Can recruit quality mentors to join their Mentor Visits.

4. Brings out the gifts of their mentor teams and helps each mentor have a positive experience.

5. Adept at identifying, developing and presenting seminars that compliment their mentoring.

6. Willing to learn some of the local language.

7. Possesses significant business experience which easily translates into wise coaching.

8. Adept at forging warm, personal relationships with recipient entrepreneurs.

9. Committed to giving difficult-to-hear advice that will help businesses grow.

10. Perceives cross-cultural dynamics and translates business principles into culturally-appropriate forms.

# Mentor Recruiting Steps

## (not in prescribed order)

- Identify a personal list of potential candidates from your own network and approach each one.

- Share your passion for the organization.

- Explain how our programs work.

- Explain the financial commitment required to be an international mentor.

- Give a free copy of GrowBook and explain how it is used in our mentoring and training.

- Learn about a potential candidate's business experience and accomplishments to determine whether he/she has the acumen to coach effectively.

- Have candidate fill out international mentor application.

- Invite current international mentors to share stories of impact and relationship.

- Connect candidate with lead mentor and/or executive director.

- Share recent stories and photos of programs in their countries (or regions) of interest.

- Give a free copy of Mentor Tools and suggest a few tool for them to read.

- Suggest reading for growth from our Recommended Reading list.

- Discuss our Best Practices of International Mentors.

- Discuss vision/mission/values to determine alignment. Explain our by-law regarding our Christian foundation.

- Invite to attend and/or volunteer at Paddle Out Poverty each April.

- Invite potential candidate to observe or volunteer in our Florida program – teaching a seminar or mentoring a local entrepreneur.

- Add candidate to email newsletter list.

- Give candidate the annual travel calendar and ask if any of the trips are possibilities for them.

- Ensure candidate's passport is current.

- Identify the challenges the candidate faces in becoming a mentor and discuss ways to overcome those barriers.

- Take one of these steps with the candidate each month, meeting face-to-face at least quarterly.

# Screening Prospective Mentees

## Requirements for Receiving Mentorship:

A. Has five or more full-time equivalent employees.

B. Has strong potential to create many jobs within two years.

C. Eager to learn and innovate.

D. Desires to use business to serve the common good.

E. Desires to develop into a local mentor.

F. Commits to schedule of events (quarterly seminars & mentoring sessions, monthly group meetings & individual follow up).

## Interview Questions to Screen for Above Requirements:

1. How many employees and sub-contractors do you currently have? How many are full-time? How many are part-time? (A)

2. Do you want to grow your business or are you happy with its current size? (B)

3. How do you envision your business in three years, and what steps will get you there? (B)

4. How many employees or sub-contractors do you expect to add within two years? (B)

5. Tell us about a time you made a positive change in your business after hearing some constructive criticism. (C)

6. What are the most important changes you've made in your business in the past year? (C)

7. What needs in your community concern you? (D)

8. What positive impact is your business currently making in your community? (D)

9. What community impact do you expect to make five years from now? (D)

10. Would you consider becoming a local mentor in two years? (E)

11. Are you willing to meet with us quarterly for mentorship and with local staff monthly for follow up? (F)

12. Are you willing to meet with the other entrepreneurs regularly for mutual support? (F)

13. Are you willing to attend our quarterly business training seminars? (F)

# Program Fact Sheet:

This business mentoring and training program is designed to provide intellectual capital to complement the financial capital offered by _____. Creating Jobs Inc is partnering with: _____ to "mentor and train entrepreneurs to grow companies, create jobs and help communities thrive". As these entrepreneurs grow in their leadership, they grow companies which meet the needs of their communities.

## Program Goals:

1. Entrepreneurs improve their leadership in the following aspects of business management: long-term planning, branding, marketing, lead generation, sales, client fulfillment, employee management, financial management, and community renewal.

2. Companies increase their efficiency and grow their revenue.

3. Business growth catalyzes new jobs.

4. Entrepreneurs intentionally use their businesses to serve their communities.

5. Entrepreneurs begin mentoring other entrepreneurs.

## Program Method:

1. During Creating Jobs Inc's quarterly mentor visits, representatives from the collaborating organizations visit entrepreneurs at their places of business for two-hour mentoring sessions.

2. In between each quarterly mentoring session, _____ makes a follow up visit to clarify mentor recommendations, track progress on goals, and provide encouragement and accountability. A summary of these visits is given to Creating Jobs Inc through the Follow Up Form.

3. Creating Jobs Inc teaches business training seminars each quarter, using the 25 training sessions in GrowBook.

4. Entrepreneurs are encouraged to meet together monthly for informal mutual support and encouragement.

5. During (and especially after) two years of receiving mentorship, entrepreneurs are encouraged to mentor others. Mentoring sessions begin to focus not only on the entrepreneurs' own businesses but also the ones they are coaching.

6. Local mentors join international mentors to mentor entrepreneurs. Local mentors receive training quarterly and meet with each other monthly for mutual support and accountability.

## Entrepreneur Requirements:

1. Have high capacity and motivation to "grow companies, create jobs and help communities thrive".

2. Host quarterly mentoring sessions at your business, discussing the details of your business in a confidential setting.

3. After considering advice from mentors, set and pursue quarterly goals to improve your business.

4. Read GrowBook and implement what you learn using the GrowBook Action Plan.

5. Attend quarterly business training seminars and seek to implement what you learn.

6. Connect with other entrepreneurs in the program for mutual support and encouragement.

7. Be willing to grow into a mentor to other entrepreneurs.

# Hoja de Información del Programa:

Traducido por Debora Velis

Este programa de mentores de negocios y capacitación está diseñado para proporcionar el capital intelectual para complementar el capital financiero ofrecido por _____. Creating Jobs Inc se ha asociado con: _____ _____ a "dar mentoria y capacitar a los emprendedores a crecer compañías, crear empleos y ayudar a las comunidades a prosperar". A medida cada emprendedor crece en sus liderazgo, ellos crecen empresas que satisfacen las necesidades de las comunidades.

## Metas del programa:

1. Emprendedores mejoran su liderazgo en los siguientes aspectos del negocio: planificación a largo plazo, marca, mercadeo, generación de comercialización, ventas, satisfacción del cliente, manejo de empleados, manejo financiero, y transformación comunitaria.

2. Las empresas aumentan su eficiencia y crecen sus ingresos.

3. Crecimiento del negocio cataliza nuevos empleos.

4. Emprendedores utilizan intencionalmente sus negocios para servir a las comunidades.

5. Emprendedores empiezan a dar mentoria a otros emprendedores en su comunidad.

# Metodología del programa:

1. Durante las visitas trimestrales, representantes de las organizaciones visitaran en sus lugares de trabajo y empresas a los emprendedores para una sesión de dos horas de mentoria.

2. Entre cada visita de mentoria, _____ hara una visita de seguimiento para aclarar las recomendaciones del mentor, medir los avances de las metas, y proveer animo y rendicion de cuentas. Un resumen de esta visita sera presentado a traves de la "hoja mensual de seguimiento".

3. Creating Jobs Inc impartirá seminarios de negocios cada trimestre, usando las 25 sesiones de entrenamiento en GrowBook.

4. Los emprendedores serán motivados a que se reúnan con otros emprendedores para animarse y apoyarse mutuamente.

5. Durante (y especialmente después) de dos años de recibir mentoria, los emprendedores serán animados a dar mentoria a otro emprendedor. Las sesiones de mentoria iniciaran enfocándose no solo en el negocio del emprendedor sino en el negocio a quien apoyaran.

6. Mentores locales se unen mentores internacionales mentor empresarios. Mentores locales reciben capacitación trimestral y se reúnen entre sí mensual para el apoyo mutuo y la responsabilidad.

# Requisitos del emprendedor:

1. Tener una alta capacidad y motivación para "crecer empresas, crear fuentes de empleo, y ayudar a que las comunidades puedan prosperar".

2. Recibir en su negocio las visitas cada tres meses con una

duración de dos horas donde podemos hablar de asuntos confidenciales del negocio.

3. Después de considerar el consejo de un mentor, planear y trabajar en las metas trimestrales para mejorar su negocio.

4. Lea GrowBook y poner en práctica lo que se aprende mediante el GrowBook Plan de Acción.

5. Asistir a los seminarios trimestrales y buscar implementar lo que ha aprendido.

6. Conectarse con otros emprendedores del programa para apoyarse y animarse mutuamente.

7. Tener el deseo de mas adelante convertirse en un mentor para otros emprendedores.

# Metrics

Entrepreneurs Served – number of current mentees in your cohort. Include local mentors who actively run a business.

Community-Serving Businesses – number of mentees and local mentors who are intentionally bettering their employees and/or community.

Growing Businesses – number of mentee and local mentor businesses with positive year-on-year revenue growth.

Jobs Created – new jobs added by mentees and local mentors in current year (full time equivalents, part-timers counted as ½). Job loss in one business is not counted against job gains in another. Losses count against gains in the same business and reduce its 'jobs retained'.

Jobs Retained – jobs retained in current year, including business owner and spouse (if working in business). Include jobs retained by local mentors.

International Mentors – number of mentors serving your cohort this year.

Local Mentors – number of indigenous entrepreneurs mentoring others.

Entrepreneur Training Events – number of seminars your cohort had access to.

Entrepreneur Training Participants – number of attendees at those seminars.

# Part Five:

---

TRIP LOGISTICS

LOGÍSTICA VIAJE

PLANIFIKASYON POU VWAYAJ

# Packing List for Six Day International Trip

**Clothes (male):**
1 khaki shorts

2 athletic shorts

1 pair athletic socks

5 pair dress socks

I athletic shirt

2 colored t-shirts

6 underwear

4 khaki pants

5 golf shirts

**Wear on airplane:**
Jeans

Golf shirt

Belt

Shoes/socks

**Bring:**
Pillow

$150 cash to Haiti, $100 to Honduras including small bills for tips at restaurants and hotel.

Passport, driver's license, credit card (with copies of each)

Flight itinerary – check in online with Copa

8 Granola bars to eat/share

2 bags of pistachios

M&Ms & chocolate bar

Frisbee/soccer/pump

Earplugs

Toiletries including sanitizer, sunscreen, shampoo, wet wipes

Whole bag of Ricola, vitamins, sickness pills

Phone & chargers

Dry erase marker

Training/mentoring handouts, included translated ones

2 kitchen trash bags

Sunglasses

Satchel

Clipboard

Mentor Tools & GrowBooks in local language

Reading: one magazine & Kindle on phone for bible & books

Thermos

Business cards

## Do before trip:
Call bank to authorize international charges to debit card.

Make out of office messages for phone and email.

Give trip schedule to family member.

Write on notecard and put in passport: name/address/phone of hotel, flight number.

# Creole Phrase Guide

**First Visit:**

| English: | Kreyol: | Notes: |
|---|---|---|
| Good afternoon, sir. | Bonswa misye. | |
| Good morning, ma'am. | Bonjou madam. | Used to address a middle-aged or older woman. |
| Excuse me, miss. | Eskizem madmwazèl. | Used to address young woman presumed to be single. |
| Yes, please. | Wi, silvouplè. | |
| Thank you very much. | Mèsi bokou. | |
| Thank you for everything. | Mèsi pou tout bagay. | |
| Goodbye my friend. | Orevwa zanmi mwen. | |
| See you next time. | Na wè ou yon lot fwa. | |
| With pleasure. | Avèk plezi. | Say after being introduced to someone. |
| What's your name? | Kouman ou rele? | |
| My name is…. | M' rele…. | |
| What's new? | Sa k pase? | Common greeting among friends. |

| English: | Kreyol: | Notes: |
|---|---|---|
| Where do you live? | Ki kote ou rete? | |
| How are you? | Kouman ou ye? | |
| Not too bad. | Pa pi mal. | Common answer to "How are you?" |
| I'm fine. And you? | Anfòm. E ou menm? | |
| How is your family? | Kouman fanmi ou ye? | |
| How is your business? | Kouman bizniz ou ye? | |
| Good work! | Bon travay! | |
| God bless you. | Bon Dye beni ou. | |
| How do you say…? | Kijan yo di…? | |
| What did you say? | Ki sa yo di? | |
| Do you speak English? | Ou pale anglè? | |
| A little bit. | Pitipiti. | Used to say you know a tiny bit of a language. |
| I'm hungry. | M' grangou. | M' is a contraction of mwen which means I. |
| Beautiful/good/well | Bèl/bon/byen | |
| Okay. | Dakò. | |

**Second Visit :**

| English: | Kreyol: | Notes: |
| --- | --- | --- |
| He/she will come today. | Li pral vini jodi a. | Pral is used to indicate future tense. |
| He/she went to church. | Li te ale legliz. | Te indicates past tense. |
| We are going to church. | Nou ale lekòl. | Nou means we, us, our, you, your |
| How did you sleep? | Kouman ou te' domi? | |
| I would like a bottle of water | M' ta renmen yon boutèy dlo. | |
| I want to buy peanuts. | M' vle achte pistach. | Vle is not as polite as ta renmen. |
| Are you ready? | Eske ou pare? | |
| 1/2/3/4/5 | En/de/twa/kat/senk | |
| Praise the Lord! | Beniswa letènèl! | |
| Your English is getting better. | Anglè ou vin pi bon. | |
| I'm sorry. | Mwen regrèt. | |
| Where are we going? | Kikote nou ale? | |
| You are a beautiful little girl. | Ou se yon bèl tifi. | |
| You are a strong little boy. | Ou se yon tigason fò. | |
| How much money? | Konbyen lajan? | |
| Would you like to drink something? | Eske ou ta renmen bwe yon bagay? | Eske is used when a question begins with a verb. |

| English: | Kreyol: | Notes: |
|---|---|---|
| You're crazy in the head! | Ou fou nan tèt! | |
| He's crazy. | Li tèt anba. | Literally: on it's head (upside down). |
| No problem. | Pa gen problèm. | Literally: have no problem as pa indicates negative. |
| I don't understand. | M' pa kompran. | |
| I don't know. | M' pa konnen. | |
| I am learning Creole. | M'ap aprann kreyol. | |
| I am pleased to see you again. | M' kontan wè ou anko. | |
| I am pleased to work with you. | M' kontan travay avèk ou. | |
| It costs 50 gourdes. | Li koute senkant goud. | 42 gourdes (Haiti's currency) = $1USD. |
| Why? | Pouki sa? | |
| If God wills. | Si Dye vle. | Common answer regarding future plans. |
| Thank God. | Gras a Dye. | Expression used to acknowledge something good that's happened. |
| We will leave tomorrow. | N'ap kite demen. | |
| When is the training? | Kilè fòmasyon a? | |

Learn more Creole at HaitiHub.com

# Spanish Phrase Guide

| English | Spanish | Pronunciation |
|---|---|---|
| Good morning. | Buenos días. | booEHN-os DEE-as |
| Good afternoon. | Buenas tardes. | booEHN-as TAR-dehs |
| Good evening. (greeting) | Buenas noches. | booEHN-as NO-chehs |
| Hello, my name is John. | Hola, me llamo Juan. | OH-la meh YA-mo Wahn |
| What is your name? | ¿Cómo se llama usted? | KOH-moh seh YA-mah oos-TEHD |
| How are you? | ¿Cómo está usted? | KOH-moh ehs-TA oos-TEHD |
| I am fine. | Estoy bien. | ehs-TOY bee-EHN |
| Nice to meet you. | Mucho gusto. | MOO-choh GOOS-toh |
| Goodbye. | Adiós. | ah-dee-OHS |
| See you later. | Hasta luego. | AHS-ta looEH-go |
| I am lost. Where is the restroom? | Estoy perdido. ¿Dónde está el baño? | ehs-TOY pehr-DEE-doh. DOHN-deh ehs-TA el BAH-neeo |
| Excuse me. | Con permiso. **OR** Perdóname | kohn pehr-MEE-soh **OR** pehr-DOH-nah-meh |
| Please. | Por favor. | pohr fah-VOR |

| English | Spanish | Pronunciation |
|---|---|---|
| Thank you. | Gracías. | gra-SEE-ahs |
| I'm sorry. | Lo siento. | low see-EHN-to |
| Bless you. | Salud. | sah-LOOD |
| You are welcome (it was nothing). | De nada. | deh NA-da |
| How much does it cost? | ¿Cuánto cuesta? | kooAN-to KWEHS-ta |

Source: www.learnspanishtoday.com where many more phrases can be found.

# Part Six:

---

BUSINESS AS MISSION

NEGOCIOS COMO MISIÓN

BIZNIS TANKOU MISYON

# Recommended Reading

## SELF LEADERSHIP

**The Holy Bible**
*Various authors*
Provides worldview of good but broken world and our part in its restoration.

**The Seven Habits of Highly Effective People: Powerful Lessons in Personal Change**
*Stephen Covey*
Finding your direction in life and pursuing it effectively.

## ORGANIZATIONAL LEADERSHIP

**Lincoln on Leadership: Executive Strategies for Tough Times**
*Donald Phillips*
A leader who is rich in character, listens long, shares the risks of his people, leads by
example, and orchestrates strong results from a talented but unruly team.

**First, Break All the Rules: What the World's Greatest Managers Do Differently**
*Marcus Buckingham & Curt Coffman*
Incisive insight into cultivating employee engagement.

## BUSINESS BUILDING

**GrowBook: 25 Essential Drivers of Small Business Success in the Developing World**
*Evan Keller, Jennifer Pettie, Manny De La Vega, Grace John*

Creating Jobs Inc business training curriculum honed in developing-world contexts.

**E-Myth Mastery: The Seven Essential Disciplines for Building a World Class Company**
*Michael Gerber*
Identifying and explaining the major systems needed in every strong company.

**From Good to Great: Why Some Companies Make the Leap... and Others Don't**
*Jim Collins*
Classic text which includes several essential principles for building strong organizations.

# CAUSES OF WORLD POVERTY

**The Bottom Billion: Why the Poorest Countries are Failing and What Can Be Done About It**
*Paul Collier*
Four development traps that contribute to the poverty of nations.

**Why Nations Fail: The Origins of Power, Prosperity, and Poverty**
*Daron Acemoglu & James Robinson*
Economic and political institutions either extract or build a nation's wealth.

**The Central Liberal Truth: How Politics Can Change a Culture and Save It from Itself**
*Lawrence Harrison*
Cultural values strongly influence a nation's progress.

# SUSTAINABLE SOLUTIONS
# TO WORLD POVERTY

**Walking with the Poor: Principles and Practices of Transformational Development**
*Bryant Myers*
Holistic poverty alleviation approaches built on decades of research and practice.

**When Helping Hurts: How to Alleviate Poverty Without Hurting the Poor...and Yourself**
*Steve Corbett & Brian Fikkert*
Building on the strengths and dignity of the poor.

# ROLE OF BUSINESS IN
# POVERTY ALLEVIATION

**Why Business Matters to God**
*Jeff Van Duzer*
The biblical purpose of business and its role in human flourishing.

**The Poverty of Nations: A Sustainable Solution**
*Wayne Grudem & Barry Asmus*
A theologian and an economist team up to show how capitalism and 35 cultural beliefs encourage economic growth.

# THEOLOGICAL UNDERPINNINGS OF
# "BUSINESS FOR GLOBAL GOOD"

**Culture Making: Recovering our Creative Calling**
*Andy Crouch*
Mimic our Creator by cultivating and creating cultural goods with eternal significance.

**Heaven is a Place on Earth: Why Everything You Do Matters to God**

*Michael Wittmer*

This world and our connection to it are far more important than we've been led to believe.

**Surprised By Hope: Rethinking Heaven, the Resurrection, and the Mission of the Church**

*NT Wright*

God's new creation of the cosmos and how all our good work contributes to it.

# CROSSING CULTURES

**American Cultural Baggage**

*Stan Nussbaum*

What Americans don't realize about themselves that is obvious to everyone else.

**Foreign to Familiar**

*Sarah Lanier*

An overview of cultural differences and how to bridge them.

## Recipe: Business for Good

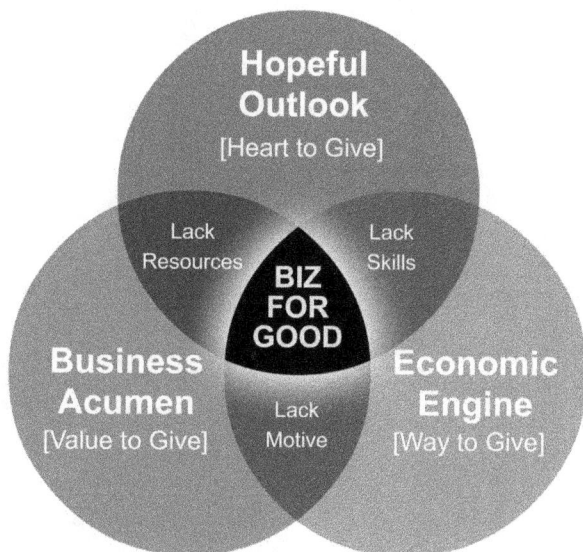

**RECETA: NEGOCIOS PARA EL BIEN**

Perspectiva llena de Esperanza
[Corazón para Dar]

Falta de Recursos

Falta de Habilidades

Negocios para el Bien

Visión de Negocios
[Valor para Dar]

Falta de Motivo

Motor Económico
[Manera de Dar]

## Fòmil: Biznis pou Byen

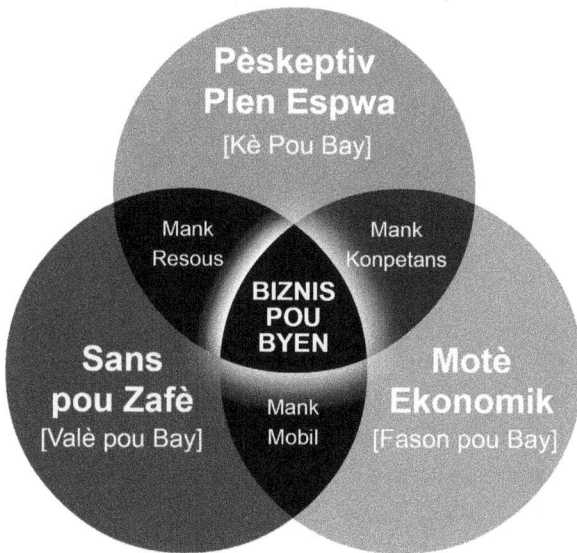

Pèskeptiv Plen Espwa
[Kè Pou Bay]

Mank Resous

Mank Konpetans

BIZNIS POU BYEN

Sans pou Zafè
[Valè pou Bay]

Mank Mobil

Motè Ekonomik
[Fason pou Bay]

# Foundational Documents
# of Creating Jobs Inc

## Vision:

Business for Global Good.

## Mission:

Mentor and train entrepreneurs to grow companies, create jobs, and help communities thrive.

## Values:

1. **Business as a Force for Good**: Innovative entrepreneurs create revenue, jobs, and needed products and services. The resulting economic multiplier effect can break the cycle of poverty for entire communities. Productive, creative work adds purpose and dignity, which contributes to human flourishing.

2. **Capacity Building**: Entrepreneurs are eager to receive and pass on the high-impact investment of intellectual capital. As business acumen is shared in the context of long-term friendships, local business leaders are cultivated and lead the way in addressing the needs of their communities.

3. **World-Class Curriculum**: With input from our recipients, we continually develop and perfect our business training curriculum and our mentoring processes.

4. **Biblical Justice and Compassion:** Our work is propelled by

God's heart for the poor as expressed in the Mosaic Law's protection of the powerless, in the cry of the prophets for justice, and supremely in Jesus who healed the sick and announced that his reign of justice and wholeness is coming "on earth as it is in heaven," bringing spiritual, social, ecological, and economic renewal, of which our work is a foretaste.

5. **Cross-Worldview Teamwork**: While operating from a biblical foundation, we intentionally involve people of various worldviews and prize the multiplied impact of our diverse partnership.

# Biblical Basis of Creating Jobs Inc's Mission

Since Creating Jobs Inc's focus is somewhat unique, some may wonder whether it's truly a Christian mission worthy of support alongside more traditional missions activity. Creating Jobs Inc is an unapologetically Christian organization, with "Biblical Justice and Compassion" as the core value which explains the impetus for our work. Non-Christians are invited to share their business acumen alongside us as long as they agree to not work against our Christian foundation. While direct evangelism is not a stated purpose of Creating Jobs Inc, it is my eager expectation that it will continue to be a central feature of the Christian/non-Christian interactions which Creating Jobs Inc affords. Too often we are isolated in our Christian "bubble", preventing non-Christians from seeing lives and communities which actively reflect Jesus by loving neighbors "that they may see your good works and glorify your Father which is in heaven". This salt-and-light effect is already central to Creating Jobs Inc, opening up many gospel conversations and entire new Christian/non-Christian relationships! Prayer and the biblical foundations of business are explicit in our work, but public altar calls are not. Nevertheless, I do believe that communicating the gospel and calling others to follow Jesus remains **the primary calling of every believer**, and Creating Jobs Inc provides the context of long-term, trusting relationships in which gospel-sharing can flourish. Isolation from non-Christians is one of the biggest roadblocks to evangelism, and Creating Jobs Inc involves non-Christians (unwittingly) in a Kingdom of God purpose! But even aside from the direct evangelism that happens in the context of Creating Jobs Inc relationships, I believe that our work of creating jobs for the poor is a part of the church's mission. To explain why requires the theological foundation which follows.

I believe the "Missio Dei" (God's mission) can be summed up as "glorifying God by reconciling all things to himself": "For God was pleased to have all his fullness dwell in [Christ], and through him to reconcile to himself all things, whether things on earth or things in heaven, by making peace through his blood, shed on the cross" (Colossians 1:19-20). This is central to God's purposes in the world and will reach its consummation at Christ's return when Revelation 11:15 is fulfilled: "The kingdom of the world has become the kingdom of our Lord and of his Christ, and he will reign for ever and ever." That day will mark the answer to the Lord's Prayer "your Kingdom come, your will be done, on earth as it is in heaven". From thenceforth, "the earth shall be filled with the knowledge of the glory of the LORD, as the waters cover the sea" (Habakkuk 2:14). Wow! It's going to be absolutely awesome! A famous quote by theologian Abraham Kuyper revels in the completeness with which the universe will submit to Christ's beatific reign: "There is not a square inch in the whole domain of our human existence over which Christ, who is Sovereign over all, does not cry: 'Mine!'" He wants it all! God will renew and redeem everything: souls, societies, economies, families, friendships, churches, law enforcement, departments of justice, arts & culture, sports, science, politics, governments, schools, businesses, and the natural order when "the creation itself is liberated from its bondage to decay and brought into the glorious freedom of the children of God" (Romans 8:21). All that is broken and evil will give way to righteousness, justice and shalom.

Not only does this characterize our future with God, but it is to loom large in our present walk with God and our work in the world. Christ's resurrection was the greatest in-breaking of God's rule in the history of the world, and his Spirit-empowered Church is to be a sign and foretaste of the Kingdom of God in everything she is and does. Since God is on mission to redeem every aspect of human life and society, His people are to be used by Him to offer a glimpse of what every corner of the universe will look like when it is fully restored to God's original intention. With the Fall of Adam, theologians tell us (with some variation) that four fundamental human relationships were broken: with God (the primary one, and thus the primacy of evangelism), with self, with others, and with the rest of Creation. In fact, Bryant Myers (of World Vision in his important book <u>Walking With the Poor</u>) defines poverty as brokenness in these four areas of life. Author Mark Russell writes that "God is on a mission to reconcile all four realms of brokenness." He acknowledges the primacy of restoring relationship with God, then writes: "However, in many places, there is no direct talk about healing the other three areas of brokenness or any acknowledgement that this necessary healing is also part of the mission to which God has called us. And even when there is that recognition, there is often an absence of any tangible, real-life solution or response" (<u>The Missional Entrepreneur</u> p.15-16). Creating Jobs Inc is one such tangible solution.

Even those who question whether the church is to transform society would readily acknowledge that how Christians act outside the church's walls is both a great witness to the gospel and alternatively a great repulsion to the gospel. So, at the very least, Creating Jobs Inc will be a powerful demonstration of the gospel, opening up opportunities to share the good news of God's transforming love (and already has as I've spoken to Chambers of Commerce and Rotary Clubs and secular university classes in Florida and Honduras). "The world is meant to see and know something about God through the lives and actions of faithful worshipers. As we live out, carry forth, and demonstrate in character and action the life of the One we worship, they see God" (Mark Labberton, <u>The Dangerous Act of Worship</u> p.37). I recall the day we did (at no charge) thousands of dollars worth of dangerous tree work in the blistering heat for a Hurricane Katrina victim in New Orleans. This ailing and aging non-Christian said through his tears: "It's as if God was in my backyard today." His unbelief didn't last long! His conversion is a perfect example of the following quote from the Lausanne Cape Town Commitment: "...our social involvement has evangelistic consequences as we bear witness to the transforming grace of Jesus Christ."

Recall the Great Commandment to love our neighbor and the 2000 verses of Scripture which reveal God's heart for the poor and our responsibility to "act justly" toward them. This places Creating Jobs Inc's work squarely within the biblical mandate for his people. One of the most important roles of the church is to "enable men and women to function within the secular life of the world in ways which reflect the reality of Christ's passion and thereby make the reality of Christ's resurrection credible" (Leslie Newbigin, <u>Sign of the Kingdom</u> p.58). Is business development a mission of the church? Jesus states our mission quite clearly in his prayer in John 17. Verse 18 in Wuest's translation reads: "Even as you sent me off on a mission into the world, so I sent them off on a mission into the world." New Testament scholar FF Bruce comments on this verse: They not merely remain in the world because they can do nothing else: they are positively sent into it as their Master's agents and messengers." As the church is sent *outside* the church, there it ironically discovers its true purpose. Paulo Coelho wrote: "The ship is safest when it's in port. But that's not what ships were made for." Remember that God's reign will invade every crack and crevasse of our world, including the world of business. He wants his glory to shine through it all! The "Wheaton Declaration on Business as Integral Calling" states in part that "Business can be an integral calling to proclaim and demonstrate the Kingdom of God by honoring God, loving people, and serving the world." Creating Jobs Inc helps developing-world businesses fulfill their Kingdom purpose of providing meaningful work for people that restores their dignity as God's image-bearers. Creating Jobs Inc also helps American businesspeople to see their business skills as useful beyond making a living, and that what they do every day – what they're best at – can be powerfully used of God both at home and abroad. Will you help us help businesspeople to "deploy their company's assets and competencies to help solve some of the biggest challenges facing our world today"? (p.101 <u>Why Business Matters to God</u> by Jeff Van Duzer)

www.ingramcontent.com/pod-product-compliance
Lightning Source LLC
Chambersburg PA
CBHW050946030426

42339CB00007B/316